MARITIME ENERGY MANAGEMENT IN GREECE BY THE USE OF GREEN PRACTICES AT GREEK PORTS

By: Mustafa Nejem

ABSTRACT

This research is about the green shipping practices at Greek ports where it is considered that LNG bunkering and shore power should be implemented at the ports. These initiatives are a form of using alternate fuel and maintaining renewable power sources at ports. In order to know about the efficacy and need for implementing these changes, a comprehensive literature review is conducted where various sources are reviewed based on the themes. The research review emphasized the gap in studying these factors, and then a statistical primary study was conducted. For this purpose, a t-test and ANOVA variance test is applied to data collected from 30 participants who answered the survey. The findings suggest that few green practices are implemented at Greek ports due to cost issues, maintenance problems, and leakage spills. Therefore, there is a need for Greek ports to properly strategize their management and implement the guidelines of net zero economy effectively to meet international standards and reduce the impact of pollution on marine life and its surroundings.

Keywords: maritime, energy management, Greece, Greek ports, green practices, shore power, LNG bunkering, and efficiency.

DEDICATION

To,

Selinus University Business School

I extend heartfelt gratitude for the unparalleled opportunities, mentorship, and knowledge you've bestowed upon me as a dedicated DBA student. Your unwavering commitment to excellence has been a guiding light on my academic journey. May the skills and wisdom gained here continue to shape my career, and may I carry the torch of your esteemed legacy forward.

With deepest appreciation,

TABLE OF CONTENT

LIST OF TABLES

Chapter 1

INTRODUCTION TO THE STUDY

The adoption of environment-friendly practices in ports around the world has gained significant momentum in recent years. It is a response to the growing concerns over climate change and environmental degradation. Greek ports are vital components of the trade and transportation of the country's infrastructure that have also embarked on this transformative journey towards sustainability. This study is conducted to evaluate the extent to which environmentally friendly practices include shore power, liquefied natural gas (LNG) bunkering, and emissions reduction technologies adopted in Greek ports and assess their impact on energy efficiency and emissions reduction. Greek ports are essential hubs for domestic and international maritime trade that facilitate the movement of goods and passengers. However, their operations traditionally relied heavily on fossil fuels that contribute to greenhouse gas emissions and air pollution. In response to global environmental concerns and international regulations, Greek ports have begun adopting sustainable practices that aim to reduce their carbon footprint and enhance energy efficiency. For example, shore power allows vessels to connect to onshore electrical grids while berthed, reducing the need for auxiliary engines and lowering emissions (Qi et al., 2020). In contrast, LNG bunkering provides a cleaner alternative to conventional marine fuels, significantly decreasing sulfur and particulate matter emissions. In this regard, emissions reduction technologies encompass a range of measures that include exhaust gas cleaning systems, i.e., scrubbers and the use of cleaner fuels that aim to mitigate the environmental impact of maritime activities (Al-Enazi et al., 2021). The adoption of these practices in Greek ports is of paramount importance, not only to comply with international environmental regulations but also to safeguard the natural beauty and ecological integrity of coastal regions and islands of Greece. Furthermore, these sustainable initiatives can result in improved energy efficiency, cost savings for port operators, and enhanced competitiveness on the global stage. So, this chapter circumscribes the background, problem statement, purpose, research question, and theoretical foundations of this research that explain the key ideas, definitions, assumptions, scope, delimitations, and limitations of the study. This sets the basis for conducting this research while exploring the positive impact of green ports on maritime energy management in Greece.

Introduction

Maritime energy management is an important aspect of sustainable port operations that involves the strategic planning and implementation of measures for optimizing energy use within the maritime industry. Adopting green shipping practices at Greek ports plays a pivotal role in achieving efficient energy management and reducing environmental impact. Green shipping practices comprise a range of initiatives aimed at minimizing the environmental footprint of vessels and port operations. In the case of Greek ports, several key practices have been increasingly embraced, such as shore power, LNG bunkering, emission reduction technologies, measures of efficiency, and waste management. Firstly, Greek ports have started investing in shore power infrastructure that allows ships to connect to onshore electrical grids while berthed (Prousalidis et al., 2017). This enables vessels to turn off their engines through reduction in greenhouse gas emissions and local air pollution in port areas. Secondly, Greek ports have facilitated the adoption of liquefied natural gas (LNG) as a cleaner marine fuel, where LNG bunkering infrastructure and services have been developed to support ships using this environmentally friendly alternative to conventional fuels. This initiative of Greek ports results in reduced emissions of sulfur oxides (SOx) and particulate matter. Thirdly, Greek ports have also used emission-reduction technologies like exhaust gas cleaning systems and low-sulfur fuels (Zannis et al., 2022). These technologies help vessels comply with stringent emissions regulations, improving air quality in and around ports. Fourthly, Greek ports are focused on energy-efficient practices and technologies that include improved vessel traffic management, optimized cargo handling, and energy-efficient lighting and equipment within port facilities (Sdoukopoulos et al., 2019). These energy-efficient measures enhance energy efficiency while reducing operational costs. Lastly, effective waste management practices such as recycling and proper disposal of hazardous materials are vital to reduce port activities' environmental impact and enhance sustainability. This study delves deeper into the specific green shipping practices adopted by Greek ports in the Mediterranean region and their implications for energy management and emissions reduction by examining these initiatives' strategies, challenges, and outcomes.

Background of the Study

The background for green maritime energy management is divided into seven phases. This type of management has gained eminence over the years due to increased demands about the maritime industry's environmental aspect. The key practices that have been opted over the years in the maritime industry are diverse and emerging. Before the 21st century, in the pre-2000s, people started speculating about environmental concerns, where the maritime industry mainly focused on the economic and operational aspects of ports. At this time, the vessels mainly relied on the use of conventional fuels that would affect the environment greatly. A few people at this time were troubled by the emissions of the fuels, but the consideration went unnoticed, and the management staff ignored the consequences of air and water pollution. The only change made before the 2000s was maintaining continental shelf and setting territorial sea limits that help manage offshore oil and gas (Nyman, 2015). The second phase is the rise of environmental awareness that started in the early 2000s as people started to accept that environmental sustainability is the key to survival since issues like air pollution, greenhouse gas emissions, and oil spills drew attention to the negative environmental impacts of maritime transport (Axel, 2011). At this stage, environmentalists and policymakers started to develop different initiatives. The third phase occurred in the mid-2000s when emission regulations were developed by the International Maritime Organization (IMO). The IMO's MARPOL Annex VI has established limits on sulfur and nitrogen oxide emissions, becoming a significant milestone (Leary, 2020). The regulation of IMO prompted the adoption of emissions-reduction technologies such as scrubbers and the use of low-sulfur fuels. The fourth phase is the main transitionary phase that involves the use of green technologies between the late 2000s and early 2010s, where research and development efforts led to the implementation of green technologies in the maritime sector. Shore power and LNG as alternative marine fuel gained attention during this period as Greek ports, like other ports, began exploring and implementing these technologies for reducing emissions and improving air quality in port areas. The fifth phase was to integrate the sustainable practices designed in the practical scenario, done by the mid-2010s. The green shipping practices for the ports include energy-efficient vessel design, renewable energy integration, and advanced energy management systems that have gained prominence. In this regard, Greek ports are also influenced by international trends and regulatory pressures such that they began integrating these practices into their operations. The sixth phase is ongoing innovative research that started in the late 2010s to optimize green maritime energy management. Research has examined the economic feasibility, environmental benefits, and challenges associated with adopting green practices at ports (Serra & Fancello, 2020). They have also explored the potential of emerging technologies like hydrogen fuel cells and battery-electric propulsion to reduce maritime emissions further. The last phase is post-COVID-19 sustainability acceleration in the 2020s since the maritime operations were disrupted, so the break provided an opportunity to reevaluate and accelerate sustainability efforts (Tang et al., 2021). Ports and shipping companies globally have sought ways to build back better as they emphasize sustainable and resilient practices. Hence, the importance of green maritime energy management has evolved over time, driven by increased environmental awareness, regulatory changes, and technological advancements. It is found that practices like shore power, LNG bunkering, emissions reduction technologies, and energy-efficient operations have emerged as critical strategies to reduce the environmental impact of the maritime industry, where Greek ports actively participate in these efforts. Therefore, ongoing research informs and reshapes the transition toward more sustainable maritime practices.

Problem Statement

The maritime industry at Greek ports faces a pressing environmental challenge due to its significant contribution to air and water pollution, greenhouse gas emissions, and the degradation of coastal ecosystems. This problem necessitates urgently adopting green practices to mitigate its adverse impact and transition towards sustainable port operations for maritime energy management. The urgent adoption of these practices is due to the environmental conditions. According to the World Health Organization (WHO), air pollution around Greek ports is a severe concern where high levels of sulfur dioxide (SO_2), nitrogen oxides (NOx), and particulate matter (PM) emissions from ships and port activities contribute to poor air quality (Mentese & Selçuk, 2022). This reduced air quality affects the respiratory and cardiac health of residents and workers in port areas. According to IQ air, in the area of Pireaus, particulate matter is the main pollutant that exists at $14.4\mu g/m^3$ in the air, while the concentration of SO_2 and CO is $5\mu g/m^3$ and $1.3\mu g/m^3$ respectively (IQAir, 2023). Secondly, Greek ports are responsible for a substantial share of the country's greenhouse gas emissions. Research from the European Environment Agency (EEA) implied that maritime transport accounts for approximately 5% of the European Union's total GHG emissions (Adamowicz, 2022). Greek ports contribute significantly to these emissions, and without mitigation efforts, there is a chance for these emissions to rise. Moreover, the discharge of ballast water and the release of pollutants from shipping activities can harm marine ecosystems in and around Greek ports, where the Hellenic Centre for Marine Research has shown contaminants in coastal waters that have affected aquatic life and biodiversity. Furthermore, as a member of IMO, Greece is obligated to adhere to international regulations that aim to reduce emissions and protect the marine environment. The MARPOL Annex VI regulations of IMO have set limits on sulfur emissions that require the use of cleaner fuels. If Greek ports observe non-compliance with these regulations, it can result in penalties and a tarnished international reputation that affects maritime trade. Another important reason to endorse green practices is the fact that Greek ports are gateways for trade between Europe, Asia, and Africa, where these practices can enhance their competitiveness to attract environmentally conscious shipping companies and shippers. The research has highlighted that South-East Europe has a greater potential for cost savings and increased operational efficiency through energy-efficient technologies and practices (Dimnwobi et al., 2023). Lastly, there is a growing demand for sustainable and responsible port operations by the public, local communities, and stakeholders. If the stakeholders fail to address environmental concerns, then it can lead to reputational damage and public opposition to port expansion projects. So, the adoption of green practices at Greek ports is imperative for addressing the severe environmental challenges they face, where high levels of air pollution, greenhouse gas emissions, damage to marine ecosystems, and international regulatory obligations underscore the need for immediate action. Henceforth, endorsement of sustainability not only aligns with global environmental goals but also offers economic benefits and enhances the competitiveness and reputation of Greek ports in the international maritime trade landscape.

Purpose of the Study

This research aims to conduct a comprehensive assessment of green shipping practices at Greek ports. The study seeks to examine and evaluate the extent to which environmentally friendly practices have been adopted within the Greek maritime industry. Moreover, the impact of green shipping practices is observed for these initiatives on both the local environment and the broader context of sustainable port operations. First and foremost, this research aims to provide an in-depth analysis of the current status of green shipping practices within Greek ports. This involves a thorough examination of the adoption of technologies like shore power, liquefied natural gas (LNG) bunkering, and emissions reduction strategies. Through assessment of the prevalence of these practices, different insights can be gained regarding the degree to which Greek ports have embraced sustainability in their operations. Furthermore, the research delves into the tangible effects of these green initiatives, including evaluating the reduction in air pollutants and greenhouse gas emissions resulting from implementing such practices. For this purpose, statistical analysis and measures of the environment are analysed by the use of statistical t test and ANOVA variance test along with secondary analysis through literature review. This assessment helps in knowing about the environmental benefits accrued by the Greek ports due to the implementation of green shipping efforts. Additionally, this research aims to consider the economic and competitive implications of green shipping practices for Greek ports. The research assesses the potential cost savings, energy efficiency improvements, and the ability to attract environmentally conscious shipping companies and stakeholders. Moreover, the study helps to understand the economic aspects of these initiatives that are important to demonstrate their feasibility and long-term sustainability. This research also takes into account the regulatory landscape and international commitments that Greek ports must adhere to, i.e., compliance with international regulations like MARPOL Annex VI. This adherence is essential to avoid penalties and ensure seamless global trade operations. So, the study is an evaluation of the alignment of Greek ports with these regulations and their preparedness for future environmental standards. Hence, the primary purpose of this research is to provide a holistic assessment of green shipping practices at Greek ports by examining adoption rates, environmental impacts, economic implications, and regulatory compliance. So, the study aims to shed light on the overall sustainability efforts of Greek ports and their contribution to mitigating environmental challenges while ensuring the long-term viability and competitiveness of the Greek maritime industry.

Research Question(s) and Hypotheses

The selection and option of the research question stems from the increased significance of green practices in the maritime industry, especially in the context of Greek ports. Greek ports play a pivotal role in the country's infrastructure, trade, and transportation, making their environmental impact substantial. With the global initiative to reduce greenhouse gas emissions and promote sustainable practices, Greek ports are under increased pressure to adopt green initiatives to enhance maritime energy management and mitigate environmental consequences. One key motivation behind this research question is the urgent need to assess these green practices' effectiveness in Greek ports. While there is a growing awareness of their importance, it is essential to empirically evaluate whether these initiatives help achieve their intended objectives. Specifically, the research question focuses on two critical aspects, i.e., optimizing maritime energy management, reducing extra shore power usage, and increasing reliance on LNG as a cleaner fuel source.

RQ: What is the intent of efficacy of green practices at Greek ports to ensure maritime energy management and prevent the use of extra shore power and increased use of LNG?

The hypotheses are as follows:

H00: There is no significant impact of green practices at Greek ports to ensure maritime energy management, and it does not prevent the use of extra shore power and increased use of LNG.

H01: There is a significant impact of green practices at Greek ports to ensure maritime energy management, and it does prevent the use of extra shore power and increased use of LNG.

These hypotheses represent two contrasting perspectives where H00 suggests that green practices may not be having a meaningful impact on energy management and the reduction of extra shore power and increased LNG usage in Greek ports. This hypothesis acknowledges the possibility that the desired outcomes may not be achieved despite efforts for adopting green initiatives. In contrast, H01 posits that green practices effectively improve maritime energy management, prevent unnecessary use of extra shore power, and increase reliance on LNG. This hypothesis reflects the optimism that sustainable initiatives can lead to positive changes in energy efficiency and emissions reduction in Greek ports when they are aptly implemented. The research aims to empirically test these hypotheses through data collection, analysis, and evaluation of green practices in Greek ports. The results provide valuable insights into the actual impact of these initiatives that can be a source for informed policy decisions, investment strategies, and future sustainability efforts in the maritime sector. Hence, to address this research question and test these hypotheses, it is important to advance the understanding of the role of green practices in Greek port operations and their contribution to a more sustainable maritime industry.

Theoretical Foundation

Theoretical foundations are important to guide and underpin research as they provide a framework for analyzing and interpreting findings. In the context of the research on the efficacy of green practices at Greek ports, the chosen theoretical foundations include institutional theory, porter's five forces framework, and environmental management systems that serve several valuable purposes. Firstly, institutional theory examines how organizations respond to external pressures and institutional norms in the context of green practices at Greek ports, and it helps explain how these ports adapt to environmental regulations, industry standards, and societal expectations. Greek ports are influenced by various international and regional institutions and regulations such as the IMO and EU directives, making institutional theory relevant to understanding their behavior. This theory also explains the ability of organizations to strive for legitimacy to conform to the institutional pressures, which, in the case of Greek ports, adhere to green practices that can enhance their legitimacy and reputation while aligning with the broader sustainability agenda. Secondly, Porter's five forces are particularly useful for understanding the maritime industry's competitive forces. This framework helps identify factors like suppliers' bargaining power, the threat of new entrants, and competitive rivalry. This framework can be applied in this research to assess the competitive implications of green practices in Greek ports, including their impact on attracting shipping companies and stakeholders. This model also emphasizes the economic aspects of competition. It helps to analyze the cost structure, differentiation opportunities, and potential for cost savings associated with green practices at Greek ports, which can provide valuable insights into their economic feasibility and sustainability. Lastly, Environmental Management Systems (EMS) is a structured approach to managing environmental aspects within organizations. In the context of Greek ports, EMS can be used as a benchmark to evaluate the effectiveness of their green practices, where it offers to assess environmental impacts, set objectives, and implement sustainable practices. EMS incorporates performance indicators to track environmental performance by examining how Greek ports utilize EMS and related metrics to quantify the environmental improvements that result from green practices. So, the theoretical foundations of institutional theory, porter's five forces framework, and environmental management systems are selected for their relevance to the research topic and their ability to provide structured frameworks for analysis. The following is the explanation of each of these theoretical frameworks.

Institutional Theory

Institutional theory is a framework in organizational sociology and management studies presented by John Meyer and Brian Rowan. It examines how organizations respond to external pressures, norms, and expectations within their institutional environment (Jepperson & Meyer, 2021). The theory posits that organizations such as ports and maritime entities are influenced by market forces and social, cultural, and regulatory institutions that shape their behaviors and practices. Institutional theory can be applied in Greek ports where green practices are incorporated and offer different insights. This theory is highly relevant to understanding green practices adoption at Greek ports. The first reason is compliance with external pressures, as Greek ports operate within a global and regional context and are heavily influenced by international institutions such as the IMO and EU. These institutions set regulations and standards for environmental sustainability that propels Greek ports to comply with specific green practices and emissions reduction measures. The theory helps explain how these external pressures influence the decisions and actions of Greek ports to conform to these institutional norms (Kravariti et al., 2021). Another aspect of institutional theory is that Greek ports, like all organizations, seek legitimacy in the eyes of various stakeholders, including the public, customers, and regulatory bodies (Spanuth & Urbano, 2023). Adopting green practices aligns with institutional expectations where ports enhance their legitimacy and credibility as responsible and sustainable entities. This aligns with the idea that organizations strive for legitimacy through adherence to institutionalized practices and norms. Thirdly, institutional theory introduces the concept of isomorphism, which refers that the organizations imitate the practices of others in their institutional environment. When a prominent port successfully implements green practices and achieves positive outcomes in the maritime industry, it promotes Greek ports to match those practices. Lastly, Greek ports need to navigate a complex landscape of environmental policies and regulations where institutional theory helps explain how they adopt these policies and adapt their operations to ensure compliance. Ports can establish environmental management systems, invest in emissions reduction technologies, or collaborate with environmental organizations, all in response to the institutional environment in which they operate. Hence, institutional theory provides a robust framework to analyze how Greek ports respond to the institutional pressures and norms surrounding green practices and sustainability in the maritime industry.

Porter's Five Framework

Harvard Business School professor Michael E. Porter developed Porter's five forces framework. It is a strategic analysis tool widely used to assess the competitive dynamics within an industry (Porter, 2008). It identifies five key forces that shape competition and profitability that help organizations understand their industry's attractiveness and competitiveness. Porter's five forces framework offers valuable insights regarding the efficacy of green practices at Greek ports. The application of this framework is in terms of the bargaining power of suppliers, where the green practices at Greek ports include the provision of eco-friendly technologies, alternative fuels like LNG, and equipment for emissions reduction. The analysis of this force helps assess the influence of these suppliers on Greek ports. If there are limited suppliers of green technologies or fuels, then it can increase costs and affect the adoption of green practices. In contrast, if suppliers are abundant and competitive, the ports have more bargaining power, making it easier to transition to sustainable practices (Bordoff & O'Sullivan Meghan, 2022). Secondly, the bargaining power of buyers refer to the shipping companies and stakeholders who use Greek ports for their trade operations. The attractiveness of Greek ports as environmentally responsible hubs can influence their choice of port, where ports with robust green practices can have a competitive advantage to attract these buyers, impacting the ports' profitability and competitiveness. The third aspect is the threat to new entrants in the maritime industry, including the fact that Greek ports have a high barrier to entry due to the significant infrastructure and capital requirements (Sideri et al., 2021). However, green practices can influence the threat of new entrants through the use of green initiatives such as substantial investments and expertise at the existing ports that have already adopted such practices that can deter potential new entrants in the competitive landscape. The fourth aspect is the threat of substitutes for green practices like alternative transportation modes or competing ports in neighboring countries. Ports that have invested in sustainability offer advantages that make them less susceptible to competition from substitutes. For instance, reduced emissions and more eco-friendly services can make Greek ports more attractive as compared to alternative transportation options. The last force is competitive rivalry, where the framework encourages an assessment of the intensity within the industry where green practices can influence this rivalry by differentiating ports. Ports that lead in sustainability can gain a competitive edge that attracts shipping companies and cargo traffic while understanding the competitive dynamics resulting from green practices that can help Greek ports strategize for sustainable growth and profitability. Hence, incorporating Porter's five forces framework into the research provides a structured approach to analyzing how green practices impact the competitive landscape of Greek ports, allowing for a comprehensive assessment of the economic and strategic implications of adopting sustainable initiatives.

Environmental Management System

An environmental management system (EMS) is a structured framework where organizations used to manage and reduce their environmental impact systematically. It involves processes, practices, and policies designed for identifying, assessing, and controling environmental risks and opportunities within an organization. For this particular research, the efficacy of green practices at Greek ports where EMS provides a structured approach to understand and implement sustainability initiatives. EMS's application in the research concerns the structured approach to sustainability. This approach is designed to provide a systematic and structured approach to managing environmental aspects within an organization. In the case of Greek ports, implementing an EMS can help them identify and prioritize green practices like emissions reduction technologies, LNG bunkering, or renewable energy integration. It enables the ports to set clear environmental objectives and track progress toward the achievement of sustainability goals. This framework also includes mechanisms to measure and monitor environmental performance by the use of key performance indicators (KPIs). Through the application of EMS principles, Greek ports can quantitatively assess the impact of green practices on energy management, emissions reduction, and overall sustainability. Moreover, EMS often aligns with international standards and regulations per globally recognized framework for environmental management. Compliance with these standards ensures that Greek ports adhere to best practices and meet regulatory requirements. It helps ports navigate complex environmental regulations and demonstrates their commitment to environmental responsibility. Moreover, EMS encourages the identification of environmental risks and opportunities where Greek ports can use EMS to assess potential risks related to climate change, pollution, or regulatory changes. Simultaneously, they can identify opportunities for enhancing sustainability, like investments in cleaner technologies or partnerships with environmental organizations. Furthermore, EMS emphasizes engagement with stakeholders, including local communities, customers, and regulatory bodies. Greek ports can use EMS to involve stakeholders in the decision-making process related to green practices, where engaging stakeholders can enhance transparency, build trust, and ensure that sustainability initiatives are aligned with the expectations and needs of the community and industry (Jun & Kim, 2021). Lastly, EMS promotes a culture of continuous improvement where Greek ports can use EMS to continually assess the effectiveness of their green practices and identify areas for enhancement. This iterative approach ensures that sustainability efforts have evolved over time and remained aligned with the changing environmental landscape. Hence, applying an EMS to the research on green practices at Greek ports offers a structured and holistic approach to understand, implementing, and assessing sustainability initiatives. So, through the adoption of EMS principles, Greek ports can systematically manage their environmental impact, measure performance, ensure compliance, engage stakeholders and drive continuous improvement in their efforts to enhance maritime energy management and reduce environmental footprints.

Nature of the Study

The nature of this study is multi-faceted as it involves a combination of secondary findings from a comprehensive literature review, secondary findings from the analysis of case studies, and primary findings derived from a survey conducted among 30 participants who work at Greek ports. The study employs statistical tools like the t-test and ANOVA variance test for rigorous examination and validation of the formulated hypotheses. The study is initiated through the conduction of an extensive literature review that serves as a foundational component. This literature review synthesizes existing research by utilizing scholarly articles and industry reports related to green practices at Greek ports. Moreover, the secondary findings extracted from this review provide a comprehensive analysis of the theoretical underpinnings, contextual factors, and global best practices in terms of sustainability initiatives and maritime energy management. This phase of the study helps establish the theoretical framework, identify research gaps, and set the stage for empirical investigation. Furthermore, the secondary findings are also derived from the analysis of relevant case studies where these case studies focus on specific Greek ports that have implemented green practices. Through the explicit examination of the findings, valuable insights are gathered from real-world examples of sustainable initiatives, their challenges, and the outcomes achieved. The analysis of case studies provides a qualitative dimension to the research that enriches the context and illustrates the practical application of green practices in Greek ports. This research also provides primary analysis that involves the collection of data from the survey among 30 participants at Greek ports. This primary research phase is instrumental in assessing green practices' effectiveness and impact at Greek ports. The research participants include port managers, environmental officers, employees, and stakeholders who are directly involved in or affected by sustainability initiatives. The survey questionnaire is designed to gather quantitative data on various aspects of green practices, energy management, and their outcomes. This data is then rigorously tested to formulate the hypothesis where the study has employed statistical analysis techniques, including the t-test and ANOVA variance test. The t-test is utilized for comparing means between two groups that assess the significance of green practices' impact on specific variables like energy management or the use of shore power and LNG (Moody-Marshall, 2023). Furthermore, the ANOVA variance test extends this analysis to assess the impact across multiple groups or factors, enabling a more comprehensive understanding of the relationships and differences between various variables. So, the nature of the study is a multifaceted endeavor that combines secondary findings from the literature and case studies with primary data collected through surveys where the data is tested through t-test and ANOVA variance that ensures a robust and holistic investigation into the complex dynamics of sustainability initiatives and maritime energy management of Greek ports.

Definitions

The keywords of this paper include green practices, maritime energy management, efficacy, shore power, LNG bunkering, emission reduction technologies, institutional theory, porter's five forces, energy management system, and greek ports. Each of these key terms is assessed, and their definitions in the context of this research are as follows:

Keyword	Definitions
Green practices	It is a practice to create structures and use processes that positively affect the environment along with a resource-efficient development cycle (Suganthi, 2019).
Maritime energy management	The use of technology and modern means to manage the shipyards and ports guarantees sustainability in terms of use of resources, environment, and cost (Fang & Wang, 2021).
Efficacy	The intent of the action or implementation of the practices that can result in a particular outcome.
Shore power	A technology that allows ships to connect to onshore electrical grids while berthed enables them to turn off their engines and reduce emissions (Wu & Wang, 2020).
LNG bunkering	The process to supply liquefied natural gas (LNG) as a cleaner and more environmentally friendly alternative fuel to ships and maritime transport for propulsion (Tvedten & Bauer, 2022).
Emission reduction technologies	Ports can employ technologies and systems like exhaust gas cleaning systems and cleaner fuels to reduce air pollutants and greenhouse gas emissions from ships and port activities (Jacyna et al., 2021).
Institutional theory	A framework used to respond to external pressures, norms, and regulatory institutions that affect their behavior and practices in sustainability (Adedoyin et al., 2022).
Porter's five forces	A strategic analysis tool used for assessing the competitive dynamics within an industry that includes factors like supplier and buyer power, the threat of new entrants, and competitive rivalry (Scott, 2020).
Energy management system	A system that is used to manage the actions, operations, environment, and finances of a project or city that aims to create energy.
Greek ports	The main focus was the ports in Greece, like Piraeus, Volos, Heraklion, Rafina, etc., to observe key practices' implementation.

Table 1 Key Definitions

These key definitions further help to know about the literature keyword strategy and clarify concepts of the topic under analysis.

Assumptions

Before conducting this study on the efficacy of green shipping practices at Greek ports, several core assumptions are made to provide a foundational framework for research and analysis. These assumptions were essential to shape the research direction and guide the investigation for the adoption and impact of sustainability initiatives in the maritime industry. The first core assumption is of the environmental awareness and responsibility that there is a growing sense of awareness regarding environmental responsibility within the Greek maritime industry. It is assumed that Greek ports recognize the urgent need to address environmental challenges like air and water pollution, greenhouse gas emissions, and damage to coastal ecosystems. The assumption explicates that there is a willingness to embrace green practices to mitigate these challenges and contribute to global sustainability goals. The second assumption is that the

Greek ports are committed to adherence to international regulations and standards related to environmental protection and emissions reduction. This assumption includes compliance with regulations set by organizations such as IMO and EU, where Greek ports are assumed to be aware of the potential penalties and reputational risks associated with non-compliance and are taking steps to meet these obligations. The third assumption is that green shipping practices like the use of LNG, emissions reduction strategies, and energy-efficient technologies are economically viable for Greek ports. It is presumed that these practices are not only environmentally responsible but also offer cost-saving opportunities in the long run, where ports are expected to consider the economic benefits of sustainability initiatives as a driving force behind their adoption. The fourth assumption is that Greek ports recognize the competitive advantage of implementing green practices, where it is presumed that ports aim to attract environmentally conscious shipping companies and stakeholders by differentiating themselves as sustainable and responsible hubs for maritime trade. Moreover, the research assumes that Greek ports actively engage with stakeholders, including local communities, customers, and regulatory bodies, in their sustainability efforts. In this case, ports are expected to value transparency and collaboration in their decision-making processes related to green practices. Another assumption is that Greek ports embrace a culture of continuous improvement in their sustainability initiatives, where ports are presumed to regularly assess the effectiveness of their green practices, identify areas for enhancement, and adapt to changing environmental conditions and technologies. The study also assumes that the implementation of green shipping practices at Greek ports can lead to a positive environmental impact. This includes the reduction of air pollutants, greenhouse gas emissions, and harm to marine ecosystems, as it is presumed that these practices effectively contribute to mitigating the adverse environmental effects associated with maritime operations. It is also assumed that there is access to reliable and comprehensive data related to the adoption and impact of green practices at Greek ports. Lastly, for the assumptions regarding primary data collection, it is assumed that participants at Greek ports are willing to participate and provide honest responses as they have a genuine interest in sharing their insights and experiences related to green practices and sustainability. Hence, these core assumptions form the foundation upon which the research on green shipping practices at Greek ports is built as they guide the research process, shape the formulation of hypotheses, and inform the interpretation of findings.

Scope and Delimitations

The scope of this study within the maritime industry of Greece is comprehensive and aims to assess and evaluate the extent to which green shipping practices and sustainability initiatives have been adopted and their impact on maritime energy management. The study focuses on Greek ports as pivotal hubs within the maritime sector, encompassing various dimensions. The first dimension is that the research examines the adoption rates of green practices in Greek ports, which includes the utilization of technologies such as shore power, liquefied natural gas (LNG) bunkering, and emissions reduction strategies. The study aims to provide an in-depth analysis of the current status of these initiatives within Greek ports that sheds light on the degree to which sustainability has been integrated into their operations. The scope of the research extends to evaluate the tangible environmental effects of green initiatives. This involves assessing the reduction in air pollutants i.e., sulfur dioxide, nitrogen oxides, and greenhouse gas emissions that result from implementing sustainability practices. The study employs statistical analysis and measures of environmental parameters for quantifying the environmental benefits accrued by Greek ports. This research also explores the economic aspects of green practices in Greek ports. It assesses the potential cost savings, improvements in energy efficiency, and the ability of these sustainability efforts to attract environmentally conscious shipping companies and stakeholders. Another scope is the evaluation of the regulatory landscape and international commitments that Greek ports must adhere to while focusing on compliance with regulations such as MARPOL Annex VI. This compliance is essential for avoiding penalties and ensuring smooth global trade operations. Lastly, the research acknowledges the importance of stakeholder engagement in sustainability efforts, where it examines how Greek ports involve local communities, customers, and regulatory bodies in decision-making processes related to green practices that help to recognize the significance of transparency and collaboration (Argyriou et al., 2022). Thus, this is the scope of this research that helps to know about the key ideas to be explored.

Despite all these aspects, there are also certain delimitations of the study. The first one is that the study focuses primarily on the Greek ports along with their specific context, where these findings might have broader relevance. However, the scope remains geographically limited to the Greek maritime industry. Secondly, the research is conducted in the paradigm of the existing case studies from the available research, where the actual primary developments are ignored. Thirdly, there is limited data available regarding green practices and their impact on maritime energy management, where data quality or access limitations could affect the depth of analysis. Moreover, the primary data collection phase involves surveys with a sample size of 30 participants at Greek ports as valuable insights are provided for this particular spectrum of the research. Lastly, though the study aims to provide insights applicable beyond Greece, the challenges and opportunities faced by Greek ports can be directly generalizable to other maritime contexts. So, these limitations are effectively replaced by the study's effective scope, and through comprehensive assessment, these delimitations are effectively addressed.

Limitations

Conducting research on the efficacy of green shipping practices at Greek ports presents several inherent limitations that impact the breadth and applicability of the research findings. These limitations encompass data availability and reliability challenges, a modest sample size that may not fully represent industry diversity, a geographic focus specific to Greek ports, constraints related to temporal considerations with a knowledge cutoff date, potential self-reporting bias in survey responses, complexities in attributing environmental impacts solely to green practices, variances in economic factors across ports, the dynamic nature of regulatory environments, the need for more comprehensive stakeholder perspectives, external influences on the industry, an emphasis on quantitative data over qualitative insights, and the difficulty in assessing the long-term sustainability and impact of green initiatives. Despite these constraints, the research remains valuable in shedding light on the state of sustainability efforts within the Greek maritime industry, serving as a foundational resource for further exploration and policy development. Researchers should maintain transparency regarding these limitations when interpreting and applying the research findings.

Significance of the Study

This study holds profound significance on multiple fronts, with its far-reaching contributions encompassing the maritime industry, environmental sustainability, and policy development. First and foremost, it addresses a pressing and critical need by meticulously assessing the adoption and real-world impact of green shipping practices within Greek ports, which are pivotal nodes within the intricate fabric of the European and global maritime network. By providing a comprehensive evaluation that quantifies not only the environmental benefits but also delves into the economic implications and regulatory compliance aspects of these sustainability initiatives, this research becomes a compass for Greek ports, guiding them towards enhancing their environmental performance while simultaneously bolstering their competitive edge in a rapidly evolving industry. Furthermore, this study harmonizes seamlessly with global imperatives concerning reducing greenhouse gas emissions and safeguarding vulnerable coastal ecosystems. It aligns itself with the overarching goals of international sustainability, making it directly relevant to global sustainability targets and objectives. The research, by shedding light on the practical implementation and outcomes of green practices, serves as a beacon of knowledge transfer and best practices dissemination, not confined solely to Greek ports but acting as a blueprint for other maritime regions seeking to embark on their own sustainability journeys. Finally, the study's findings carry immense weight in the corridors of policymaking. It provides empirical evidence and insights that are invaluable for policymakers and regulators tasked with shaping the future of maritime operations. Armed with the research's revelations on what works and what doesn't in the realm of sustainable maritime practices, policymakers can craft regulations and incentives that actively encourage and promote environmentally responsible operations. In doing so, this research paves the way for the cultivation of a maritime sector that not only adheres to rigorous environmental standards but also thrives economically, ultimately fostering a sustainable and prosperous maritime industry that safeguards our oceans and the global ecosystem.

Theoretical Significance

The three applied theories include institutional theory, porter's five forces framework, and environmental management systems (EMS), which play an important role in providing a comprehensive framework to analyze and understand the research context of green shipping practices at Greek ports. Firstly, the institutional theory is highly relevant in this research context because Greek ports operate within a complex web of international, regional, and national regulations and norms. Institutional theory helps to explain how Greek ports respond to external pressures and adapt to environmental regulations while seeking legitimacy by conforming to institutionalized practices and sustainability norms. It helps elucidate how these external forces influence the adoption of green practices by aligning the ports with global environmental goals and enhancing their reputation in the international maritime trade landscape. Secondly, Porter's framework is invaluable in assessing the competitive dynamics within the maritime industry as it aids in understanding how green practices impact the bargaining power of suppliers, i.e., eco-friendly technology providers, the bargaining power of buyers, i.e., shipping companies favoring sustainable ports, the threat of new entrants, i.e., affected by sustainability investments, the threat of substitutes, i.e., alternative transportation modes, and competitive rivalry, i.e., differentiation through sustainability. The analysis of these forces helps uncover the economic implications and strategic importance of green initiatives for Greek ports that enhance their competitiveness and attract environmentally conscious stakeholders. Lastly, EMS directly applies to the research as it provides a structured approach to managing environmental aspects within organizations. In the context of Greek ports, EMS serves as a benchmark to evaluate the effectiveness of their green practices as it helps in the systematic identification, assessment, and control of environmental risks and opportunities related to sustainability initiatives. EMS encourages using performance indicators to quantitatively track environmental improvements, which ensure that the research can measure the impact of green practices on maritime energy management, emissions reduction, and overall sustainability. Hence, these three theories collectively offer a robust analytical framework that addresses various research dimensions, including institutional influences, competitive dynamics, and the systematic management of environmental aspects.

Practical Significance

The practical significance of this research is on green shipping practices at Greek ports. It is multifaceted and holds substantial implications for various stakeholders, including ports, the maritime industry, policymakers, environmental organizations, and the broader society. The first practical significance is the critical nodes of Greek ports in global trade that stand to benefit significantly from the research findings. Through insights into the efficacy of green practices, they can make informed decisions to adopt and optimize sustainable technologies and processes, leading to cost savings through energy efficiency, reduced emissions, and better environmental performance. Moreover, it enhances its competitiveness by attracting environmentally conscious shipping companies and stakeholders, ensuring their continued viability in the global maritime landscape. Secondly, the practical significance of this research extends to environmental sustainability, as Greek ports have a substantial environmental footprint due to their maritime activities. It helps to understand the effectiveness of green practices and allows them to proactively reduce air and water pollution, greenhouse gas emissions, and the impact on coastal ecosystems. This aspect contributes to the preservation of local ecosystems, improved air quality for port workers and nearby residents while mitigating the adverse health effects of poor air quality. Thirdly, policymakers at national and international levels can leverage the research to formulate regulations and incentives that encourage sustainable maritime operations. The data-driven insights into the benefits and challenges of green practices provide a solid foundation to craft effective policies that align with global environmental goals. It ensures that Greek ports remain compliant with regulations such as MARPOL Annex VI that prepare them for more stringent standards. Moreover, the findings of the research can serve as a valuable resource to share knowledge and best practices dissemination within the maritime industry. Greek ports can share their experiences and lessons learned with other ports globally, which facilitates the adoption of green practices worldwide. This collaborative approach accelerates the transition towards more sustainable maritime operations on a global scale, which is important to address climate change and environmental degradation. Furthermore, environmental organizations and local communities can use the research findings to engage with Greek ports and hold them accountable for their sustainability efforts. In this case, transparent reporting on the impact of green practices ensures that ports align with societal expectations and demonstrate their commitment to responsible environmental stewardship. This further fosters trust and collaboration among ports and their stakeholders. Lastly, the practical significance of this research aligns with broader global sustainability goals that include those outlined in the United Nations' Sustainable Development Goals (SDGs). So, through a reduction in emissions and environmental impact, Greek ports contribute to achieving targets related to clean energy, climate action, life below water, and responsible consumption and production. Henceforth, the practical significance of this research goes beyond academic inquiry as it has real-world implications that can drive positive change in the maritime industry, protect the environment, improve public health, and advance progress toward global sustainability objectives. So, the research accentuates the transformative potential to adopt and optimize green shipping practices, making them a practical and ethical imperative for Greek ports and the wider maritime community.

Significance to Social Change

Maritime energy management holds significant implications for social change that is composed of various dimensions that can positively impact society. The social changes associated with this research are explained here. One of the most immediate and tangible benefits of effective maritime energy management is the improvement in public health, as ports and maritime activities often contribute to air pollution through the emission of harmful pollutants like sulfur dioxide (SO_2), nitrogen oxides (NOx), and particulate matter (PM). These pollutants adversely affect respiratory and cardiac health, leading to illnesses and reduced quality of life for both port workers and nearby residents. So, by implementing green practices and reducing emissions, maritime energy management can significantly enhance air quality in port areas, reducing the health risks associated with poor air quality. Secondly, ports are often located near communities, and their operations can impact the well-being of these communities in various ways. For instance, noise pollution is a common concern associated with port activities where sustainable energy management practices, like the use of shore power instead of onboard generators, can lead to quieter operations, reducing noise pollution and improving the overall quality of life for nearby residents. Additionally, reducing pollutants in the air and water contributes towards a cleaner and safer environment for communities that foster a sense of well-being and safety. Thirdly, effective maritime energy management plays a pivotal role in environmental conservation as ports are typically situated in ecologically sensitive coastal areas, and their activities can have adverse effects on marine ecosystems. For example, ballast water discharge can introduce invasive species and pollutants into local waters, disrupting the balance of marine ecosystems. Sustainable energy management practices often go hand in hand with responsible environmental stewardship that includes measures for minimizing the discharge of pollutants and the use of cleaner fuels. This contributes to the preservation of local biodiversity and marine ecosystems, which are important for the long-term well-being of the natural environment and the communities that depend on it. Moreover, the maritime industry is a significant source of employment in many regions that transition to sustainable maritime energy management practices that often involve investments in cleaner technologies, infrastructure, and workforce development. This transition can create new job opportunities in fields like renewable energy, energy efficiency, and environmental management. Moreover, the emphasis on sustainability can enhance the long-term viability of the maritime sector, which ensures the preservation of existing jobs and the creation of new, sustainable employment opportunities. Lastly, maritime energy management underscores the importance of social responsibility within the industry as ports and maritime stakeholders become more accountable for their environmental impact and take proactive steps to mitigate it. This shift towards sustainability not only improves the reputation of the industry but also fosters a culture of responsibility and accountability as it raises awareness among maritime professionals, communities, and the general public. This aspect is especially about the environmental challenges that port operations pose and the role that sustainable energy management can play in addressing these challenges. Therefore, maritime energy management is not solely an economic or environmental imperative as it is also a catalyst for positive social change through reducing pollution, improving public health, enhancing community well-being, conserving the environment, creating sustainable employment, and promoting social responsibility that contributes to a more equitable, healthy, and sustainable society.

Summary and Transition

So, this chapter has summarized the background behind conducting this study along with the problem that is elucidated for this research. After the establishment of the purpose of this study, the research questions to be assessed are explicated, followed by the theoretical implementation of institutional theory, Porter's five frameworks, and the environmental management system. Then, the nature of the study, definitions, assumptions, scope, delimitations, and limitations of the study are explained. After this, the theoretical, practical, and social significance of this research are established. Thus, the chapter has formed the basis for this research and set its background. The literature review is to be established where credible sources and case studies are assessed to know about the secondary explanation of the research question before applying primary research methodologies.

Chapter 2

Literature Review

The following is a pivotal literature review from credible sources gathered through available scholarly data. It includes a brief historical perspective, theoretical findings, conceptual framework implementation in practical scenarios, and other key case studies. This review is done thoroughly, and to ensure that none of the research selected is inaccurate, credible databases are used.

Introduction

Conduction of a thorough and credible literature review for a topic such as "green shipping practices at Greek ports" necessitates a systematic and structured approach. The steps that are to be followed for this research are explained here. The first step is already established, i.e., the establishment of research objectives that help to know about the focus of the literature review and its segments. Secondly, there is a need to identify the keywords that are explicated in the definitions and are used to search the query on the database to know about "green shipping","sustainability in maritime", "maritime energy management" and "Greek ports". So, these keywords help in locating credible resources. In this case, reputable academic databases and libraries are used to learn about maritime and green practices at Greek ports. The detail of the papers reviewed is provided in the following sections. Moreover, the search strategy is also explained in the following section before establishing the historical literature, i.e., the background for this research without a focus on Greek ports. Then, the literature search strategy is explained by using Boolean operators (AND, OR) to effectively combine keywords. The search terms are stated in the literature search strategy, which helps to know about the derived concepts. Moreover, an inclusion criteria is created to include sources within the last 5 years where all the research journals are relevant to the research question. In this case, all the sources that do not align with the research objectives are excluded. After excluding the full text of selected articles, it is retrieved to conduct a detailed review by analyzing each source's methodology, findings, and relevance by considering factors like the quality of research, sample size, and research design. The review also helps to identify the theoretical frameworks that are applicable, such as the inclusion of institutional theory, Porter's Five Forces, or environmental management systems. These frameworks help to examine how these theories are applied to the maritime industry and green shipping practices. Lastly, case studies are presented to explicate the real-world examples of green shipping initiatives at Greek ports to analyze the challenges faced, the strategies employed, and the outcomes achieved. These findings are then organized into themes or categories to summarize key findings, theoretical foundations, and practical applications. This also helps to identify gaps in the existing research that this study aims to address. Moreover, to make sure that all the articles' references remain aligned, the citation manager is used to maintain a coherent critical stance of the research articles. Thus, these steps are followed to ensure that a solid foundation is built for this research.

Historical Literature

Maritime energy management has undergone significant developments and transformations over the past 20-30 years. A growing awareness of environmental concerns, regulatory pressures, and technological advancements drives it. A brief scholarly overview is done to provide insights into key milestones and trends in the field of maritime energy management during this period.

The first phase is of environmental concerns and regulatory initiatives developed over the past few decades. According to Gössling and colleagues (2021), the increased global concern about environmental issues, including climate change and air quality, profoundly impacted the maritime industry. The review exacerbated that the shipping industry traditionally relies on fossil fuels, significantly contributing to greenhouse gas (GHG) emissions and air pollution. As a result, there has been a heightened focus on reducing maritime operations' environmental footprint. During this time, regulatory initiatives were also taken, including the MARPOL Annex VI, which states to limit the sulfur and nitrogen oxide emissions from ships. It was first adopted in 1997 and subsequently amended. According to Testa (2020), this protocol helped to establish increasingly stringent emission standards, especially in Emission Control Areas (ECAs), which include areas like the Baltic Sea and North Sea. These regulations have forced the industry to adopt cleaner fuels, including low-sulfur marine fuels and liquefied natural gas (LNG), along with implementing emission abatement technologies.

The second phase is the advancement of clean technologies in marine energy management, where the development and adoption of cleaner and more energy-efficient technologies have been instrumental in reducing emissions and improving fuel efficiency. The first key advancement is the use of LNG as a cleaner alternative to traditional marine fuels, which has gained traction (Peng, 2022). The research found that LNG-powered ships emit significantly lower sulfur oxides (SOx) and particulate matter, contributing to improved air quality. In this regard, shipbuilders have introduced more energy-efficient vessel designs that include streamlined hulls, improved engine designs, and waste heat recovery systems, where these innovations reduce fuel consumption and, consequently, emissions (de Kat & Mouawad, 2019). Moreover, some vessels have integrated renewable energy sources like wind and solar power to supplement onboard energy generation. These hybrid solutions help in the reduction of the reliance on conventional fuels.

The third phase of maritime energy management improvement is the advent of data and digitalization. The maritime industry has increasingly embraced data-driven solutions and digitalization to enhance energy management through the use of advanced monitoring and reporting systems (Kowalkowski et al., 2022). They have also made use of data analytics that enable ship operators to optimize fuel consumption and reduce emissions. This also allows real-time data analysis on engine performance, weather conditions, and voyage planning to operate the vessels more efficiently.

The fourth phase is of most eminence and the latest change i.e., Environmental Management Systems (EMS) that have gained prominence within the maritime sector. EMS frameworks are often aligned with ISO 14001 standards that provide a structured approach to managing environmental aspects within shipping companies and port facilities (Brunila et al., 2023). These systems help set environmental objectives, monitor performance, and ensure regulation compliance. Moreover, since ports are crucial nodes in the maritime supply chain, they have also undergone transformations in energy management, as many ports have integrated renewable energy sources into their operations. In this regard, shore power facilities have become more common, enabling vessels to plug into the grid while berthed to reduce emissions and noise pollution in port areas.

Irrespective of these advancements, the maritime industry has a few challenges. The industry needs further GHG emissions reductions to align with global climate goals. This requires the development and adoption of zero-emission propulsion technologies like hydrogen fuel cells and ammonia engines, which are currently in various stages of research and development to reach the idea of a net-zero economy (Bonsu, 2020). Moreover, the industry must address issues related to the availability and infrastructure for alternative fuels such as LNG and the financial investments required for green technologies. Hence, the past 20-30 years have seen significant progress in maritime energy management that is enforced by environmental concerns, regulatory actions, technological advancements, and a growing emphasis on sustainability.

Literature Search Strategy

In order to conduct the literature review efficiently, the Boolean search strategy is opted where operators like AND, and OR are used to search and find credible journals that meet the keyword criteria (Gras, 2013). Moreover, keywords are chosen based on the research question and hypothesis where not only operators but other keywords are chosen. The following table shows the operator used, topic, and the search key terms placed on the search bar.

Operator	Topic	Search Keyterm
AND	Green shipping practices	"Green shipping practices" AND "Greek ports"
AND	Green shipping practices	"Sustainable maritime operations" AND "environmental impact"
AND	Green shipping practices	"Maritime energy management" AND "regulatory compliance"
AND	Green shipping practices	"LNG propulsion" AND "emissions reduction"
OR	Theoretical frameworks	"Institutional theory" OR "maritime sustainability"
OR	Theoretical frameworks	"Port competitiveness" OR "sustainability initiatives"
OR	Theoretical frameworks	"Environmental management systems" OR "Greek ports"
	Case studies on green shipping practices	"CASE STUDIES on green practices in Mediterranean ports"
AND	Use of renewable energy	"Renewable energy integration AND maritime industry"
	Regulatory measures	"Impact of MARPOL Annex VI on Greek ports"

Table 2 Search Queries per Boolean Operators

Note that the use of inverted commas in the queries implies the extra stress on these words to ensure that all the research results have these keywords within their content.

Theoretical Foundation

The three theories that are the foundation for this research are institutional theory, porter's five forces framework, and environmental management systems (EMS). The literature on each of them in the context of maritime industry at Greek ports is discussed in this section. The first framework is institutional theory. Silva-Rêgo & Figueira (2023) focused on reviewing and mapping the existing literature on the relationship between institutional theory and Outward Foreign Direct Investment (OFDI). Since the maritime industry is a form of foreign direct investment, it helps to understand the application of the theory and its relevance. Institutional theory in international business explores formal and informal institutions like government regulations, cultural norms, and societal expectations, influencing firms' internationalization strategies and behavior (Silva-Rêgo & Figueira, 2023). It is inferred that the principles of institutional theory could be applied to the maritime industry as it operates within a complex web of international regulations, environmental standards, and cultural considerations. These institutional factors can significantly impact the shipping decisions of companies regarding their operations, route choices, and environmental practices. Thus, the theory emphasizes the institutionalization of the maritime industry based on international and environmental standards to navigate the legal and cultural complexities of operating in different regions. Another piece of literature by Lee and colleagues (2019) provides a focus on sustainability in the maritime transport and logistics industry, which represents a significant shift in stakeholder attention towards environmental and social concerns within this sector. This shift can be understood and reviewed in institutional theory, which posits that organizations and industries are influenced by formal and informal institutions that include regulations, norms, and societal expectations. The research discussed snowballing regulations imposed by the International Maritime Organization (IMO) since 1997 (Lee et al., 2019). These regulations can be seen as formal institutional pressures that have prompted the industry to address sustainability issues where they are aimed at reducing emissions, improving safety, and protecting marine ecosystems. These regulations have created a new institutional environment that shipping, which the port and maritime logistics companies must navigate. Additionally, the sustainability reflects a response to these institutional pressures, which indicates that companies adapt to their practices through seeking legitimacy by aligning with the emerging sustainability norms (Lee et al., 2019). Lastly, the findings of Galiatsatou and colleagues (2021) have proposed a methodological framework for energy management sustainability through the implementation of institutional theory. The framework assessed climate change impacts on the coastal zone and port defense structures represents a practical application of institutional theory due to environmental regulations and infrastructure management. Institutional theory posits that organizations and industries are influenced by formal and informal institutions that include regulatory frameworks and societal expectations. The research on identifying climate change impacts on coastal defense structures aligns with the formal institutional pressures stemming from international agreements and regulations addressing climate change and its consequences (Galiatsatou et al., 2021). Hence, by developing a methodology that assesses the nonstationary extreme values of sea-state parameters and their impact on coastal defense structures, the research has responded to these institutional pressures by providing a practical approach for ports to evaluate and enhance their resilience to changing environmental conditions. Porter's five framework is the second theory to be applied on this topic. According to Isabelle and colleagues (2020), Porter's Five Forces framework was introduced in 1979 and has been a valuable tool for assessing the competitiveness and attractiveness of industries. It traditionally examines five key competitive forces: the threat of new entrants, the bargaining power of buyers, the bargaining power of suppliers, the threat of substitute products or services, and the rivalry among existing competitors. However, as industries evolve and face new challenges in terms of sustainability and green initiatives, the traditional framework needs augmentation. The research explicated that the threat of new entrants could refer to the potential for environmentally conscious startups to disrupt traditional industry players, the bargaining power of buyers can consider how eco-conscious consumers can influence purchasing decisions, suppliers' power could relate to the availability of sustainable materials and technologies, substitute products or services can encompass environmentally friendly alternatives, and rivalry among competitors can involve the race to adopt and promote green practices (Isabelle et al., 2020). However, as industries become more interconnected and complex, there is a need to add forces like the competitor's level of innovativeness, exposure to globalization, the threat of digitalization, and industry exposure to de/regulation activities to capture the nuances of modern business environments, which include those shaped by green initiatives and sustainability concerns. Hence, this modification provides a more comprehensive view of how industries navigate the changing landscape, including their responses to sustainability challenges, such as reduction of environmental impact and adoption of eco-friendly practices in a post-COVID-19 world. Another article by Anastasiu and colleagues (2020) advocates for an adaptation of Porter's Five Forces Model in the realm of strategic human resources management to recognize the evolving challenges in the global business environment. These five forces are reinterpreted to emphasize their impact on human capital. Firstly, "rivalry" within the industrial sector focuses on competition among specialists with core competencies. Secondly, "organizations as buyers" highlights the demands placed on hiring companies in terms of both the number of employees and their updated skill sets. "Suppliers" refer to recruitment companies and educational institutions whose influence on human capital quality is substantial. "New entrants" are influenced by globalization and migration patterns that affect the talent pool. Lastly, "substitutes" encompass modern technologies and innovation that can alter job requirements. Hence, this adapted framework can be applied to assess the availability and suitability of human capital for environmentally responsible practices. This approach aligns with the broader goal of integrating green practices into workforce planning and development, which ensures that human capital is not only stable and of high quality but also geared towards sustainable innovation and environmental responsibility. Lastly, Rocha and colleagues' (2019) findings have applied Porter's Five Forces framework to green initiatives and sustainability. The challenges identified in the adoption of Design for Sustainability (DfS) models can be analyzed in different aspects. Firstly, the competition within industries is represented by the "rivalry" force. It is influenced by the varying approaches to DfS, where some models focus on providing a strategic vision for sustainability akin to market competition. While others offer more operational guidance i.e., resemblance to product competition. Secondly, "organizations as buyers" are concerned with the alignment of DfS models with corporate sustainability management theories i.e., akin to buyers who assess suppliers for compliance with sustainability criteria. Thirdly, "suppliers" are represented by the DfS models that offer different approaches similar to diverse suppliers that provide varying components for a product. The "new entrants" force reflects the evolving landscape of DfS adoption, with different models that enters the market. Lastly, "substitutes" can be seen as alternative approaches to integrate sustainability in design processes while competing for attention and resources within organizations. These challenges underscore the need for a harmonized and systematic approach to DfS, especially to address the social dimension, which remains relatively unestablished. The final theoretical framework is environmental management systems (EMS) where findings of Puig and colleagues (2022) suggest that environmental performance of European ports within the framework of an Environmental Management System (EMS). The study draws data from the Self-Diagnosis Method (SDM) that serves as a comprehensive checklist to enable port managers for self-assessing their environmental management practices. A total of 97 ports from 18 European Maritime States participated in this assessment that contributes to valuable insights into their environmental initiatives. The research highlights several key findings where the majority of ports have established environmental policies and compiled inventories of significant environmental aspects that underscore their commitment to sustainability. Moreover, a significant percentage of ports offer onshore power supply (OPS) and LNG bunkering that aligns with environmental objectives. Additionally, a growing number of ports incentivize eco-friendly shipping practices through differentiated dues that reflects a positive trend towards environmental improvement in the maritime industry. Another conference paper by Palantzas and colleagues (2021) explicates the significant role that small ports that include those on small islands, supply chains, transport connectivity, and local communities. Despite their smaller scale of operations, these ports face similar environmental responsibilities as larger counterparts where they must contend with legal liabilities and environmental impacts. It is often associated with fewer resources to establish and maintain effective Environmental Management Systems (EMS). However, the paper suggests that small ports can address these challenges through collaboration and knowledge-sharing within the sector by working together and leveraging their strengths. Hence, small ports can set an example through establishment of good practices and innovative ways to engage with local communities that depicts how the sector can contribute positively to its surroundings. Lastly, the findings of Bintoudi and colleagues (2020) have utilized the Ecological Footprint (EF) methodology for assessing the CO_2 emissions-related environmental impact of the port of Thessaloniki in Greece for the years 2008 and 2009. The assessment included various components of port activities like built-up land, population i.e., port staff, electricity consumption, fuel consumption, solid waste production, and wastewater production. The research explicated that the port of Thessaloniki had a relatively high total EF compared to other ports studied, especially due to elevated electricity and fuel consumption that is compounded by the higher CO_2 emission factor in the Greek electricity sector. Hence, the study underscored the potential of EF as a tool to assess environmental impact within an Environmental Management System (EMS) but also pointed out its limitations when applied to ports. In conclusion, these are the theoretical foundations that are applied on this research to know about the key ideas of maritime energy management at Greek ports.

Conceptual Framework

The conceptual framework for this research aims to investigate the impact of green practices at Greek ports to ensure maritime energy management and prevent the use of extra shore power while promoting increased use of liquefied natural gas (LNG). This framework explains theories associated with environmental sustainability, maritime energy management, and adopting green practices in the maritime industry. Firstly, the environmental sustainability theory is the foundational concept that underscores the importance of reducing greenhouse gas emissions and minimizing maritime operations' ecological footprint. This theory is aligned with the global efforts to combat climate change and protect coastal ecosystems (Martin, 2023). In this regard, sustainable maritime practices include the adoption of LNG as a cleaner fuel source that contributes to these objectives. The second concept is institutionalization, as envisaged by institutional theory, which emphasizes the role of regulations, policies, and institutional pressures in shaping organizational behavior (Ocasio, 2023). This theory explains the purpose of International Maritime Organization (IMO) regulations and national policies as driving forces for adopting green practices at Greek ports. It is found that these external institutions influence ports by implementing environmental management systems and sustainable initiatives to comply with regulations. The third concept is the resource-based view (RBV) theory, which posits that the resources and capabilities of firms can be a source of sustainable competitive advantage (Heskett, 2022). The concept explains adopting green practices like energy-efficient technologies and LNG infrastructure that represent valuable resources for Greek ports. These resources are a source of enhancing their environmental performance and competitiveness in the maritime industry. Moreover, Porter's framework in the maritime industry helps to assess the competitiveness and attractiveness of the industry. This research is focused on analyzing the bargaining power of suppliers that are LNG providers, the bargaining power of buyers i.e., shipping companies seeking eco-friendly ports, the threat of substitutes i.e., other ports that offer green services, and the competitive rivalry among ports. So, this framework provides a strategic viewpoint on the impact of green practices. The theoretical framework integrates these theories to understand the dynamics that influence the adoption of green practices at Greek ports and their impact on maritime energy management, shore power usage, and LNG utilization. The Institutional theory underscores the role of regulations and policies in driving port behavior towards sustainability. Moreover, the Resource-Based View theory emphasizes the importance of green practices as strategic resources for port competitiveness. Lastly, Porter's Five Forces Framework helps to assess the competitive landscape and the significance of green practices in attracting shipping companies. So, the research is an ongoing conversation within the maritime industry and sustainability literature as it acknowledges the increasing importance of environmental sustainability in maritime operations and aligns with global efforts to reduce greenhouse gas emissions. Additionally, it contributes to the discourse on the adoption of green practices and LNG as viable solutions for cleaner maritime energy management to address environmental concerns for achieving the goal of a net zero economy (Meys et al., 2021). Therefore, these concepts are an iterative research focus to gather the literature review and further expound on the primary analysis.

Literature Review

In order to keep the literature review succinct, the Boolean search strategy is already established. However, the literature review is divided to avoid riddling and influx of incoherent sources. In order to make different categories, the themes extracted from the background are considered. The following is a review of all the sources gathered to know about the key ideas of maritime energy management along with green shipping practices at Greek ports.

Maritime Energy Management

According to Viktorelius and colleagues (2022), a qualitative on operational energy efficiency in shipping is viewed through a sociotechnical lens. This provides valuable insights with direct relevance to the research question regarding the efficacy of green practices at Greek ports for maritime energy management. The identified themes of cooperation, communication, and knowledge sharing among stakeholders implicate collaboration's importance in effectively implementing green practices. In the context of Greek ports, the research highlights the need for coordinated efforts among port authorities, shipping companies, and other stakeholders to ensure sustainability initiatives' success (Viktorelius et al., 2022). Additionally, the organizational information processing theme explains the cognitive bottlenecks and sense-making practices within maritime organizations that emphasize the significance of decision-making processes. This is particularly pertinent to understanding how Greek ports can optimize their energy management strategies and make informed choices regarding shore power and LNG use. Lastly, the theme of professional education and training highlights human capital's critical role in driving energy efficiency improvements, which indicates that well-trained personnel are essential for successfully adopting green practices. Hence, this synthesis underscores the intricate sociotechnical dynamics that underpin energy efficiency in shipping while offering insights that can inform the development and implementation of green practices at Greek ports for the achievement of maritime energy management goals effectively and sustainably.

Another systematic review by Fan and colleagues (2021) has explained that LNG bunkering and simultaneous operations (SIMOPs) are paramount to the research question concerning the efficacy of green practices at Greek ports for maritime energy management. As the maritime industry increasingly shifts toward sustainable and green practices, LNG has emerged as a potential alternative for marine fuel due to its environmental benefits. However, the availability and safety of LNG bunkering operations are critical factors in terms of its unanimous application. The study explores LNG bunkering SIMOPs at Greek ports where efficient and safe bunkering operations are important for the successful transition to LNG as a marine fuel. So, it is essential to understand the safety philosophy and risk analysis methods as it is important for Greek ports that aim to optimize their energy management while guaranteeing that safety standards are met. The identification of research gaps in the study provides valuable insights for future investigations as it offers a roadmap to accelerate the development of safe and efficient LNG bunkering SIMOPs in Greek ports. Another article by Coimbatore Meenakshi Sundaram and Karimi (2023) also explained the eminence of LNG bunkering. They found that LNG bunkering procedures use the Technical Reference 56 (TR 56) national standard, which are highly pertinent to the research question concerning the efficacy of green practices at Greek ports for maritime energy management. The International Maritime Organization's (IMO) 2020 regulation necessitated the transition to cleaner and sustainable bunkering fuels where LNG is a prominent solution. It is because Greek ports and the wider maritime industry seek to adopt LNG as a more environmentally friendly alternative as they understand the bunkering procedures and associated costs and emissions become crucial. The study focuses on dynamic simulation and its recommendations for efficient bunkering operations like bottom-filling and purging. These aspects have direct implications for Greek ports that aim to optimize their LNG bunkering processes. Moreover, the findings emphasize the significance to adhere to established standards like TR 56 that ensure safe and environmentally responsible bunkering practices. Hence, these pieces of literature guides that Greek ports in their pursuit of green practices are aligned with international regulations that further enhances maritime energy management and reduces emissions. The concept of LNG bunkering is illustrated below.

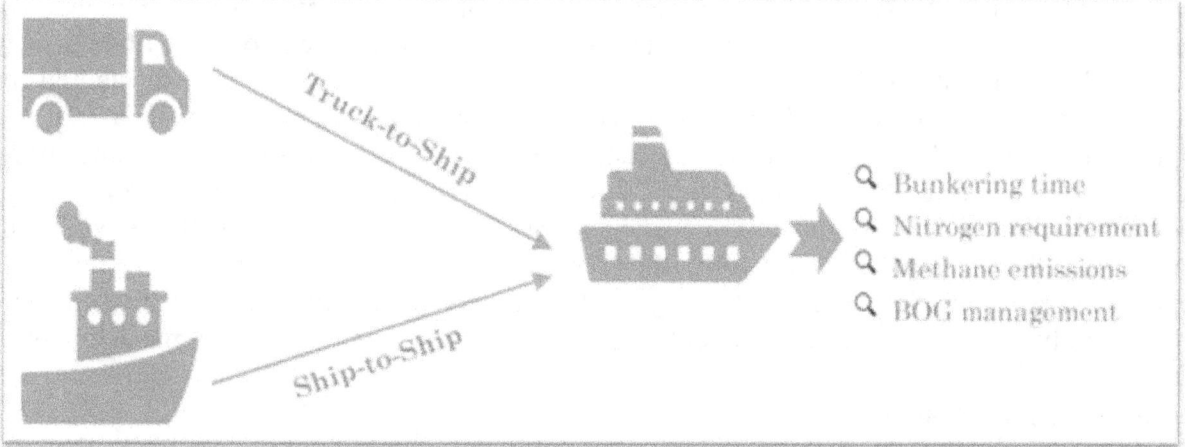

Figure 1 LNG Bunkering (Coimbatore Meenakshi Sundaram & Karimi, 2023)
In regards to LNG bunkering, there are different policies associated, as explicated by Ha and colleagues (2023). The findings of the research explored the determinants of selecting LNG bunkering ports from the perspective of liner shipping companies in South Korea. This holds significant relevance to the research question regarding the efficacy of green practices at Greek ports for maritime energy management. As the maritime industry increasingly embraces LNG as a cleaner fuel source, the selection of suitable bunkering ports becomes essential. This research has employed interpretive structural modeling (ISM) to uncover the interactive relationships among decision determinants and provides valuable insights for Greek ports that aim to enhance their green practices and maritime energy management. The identification of core determinants is categorized into basic requirements, i.e., port attractiveness and core components. These are multifaceted considerations that influence the shipping choices of companies. These findings serve as a valuable reference for policymakers and Greek ports as they offer a strategic perspective from the shipping industry and facilitate the development of effective LNG bunkering port strategies that align with green and sustainable practices in the maritime sector.

Another important aspect of maritime energy management is shore power. The study is presented by Xu and colleagues (2021) as they investigate the dynamics of strategic choices in the implementation of a shore power system involving government, port enterprises, and liner companies. It offers valuable insights into the research question concerning the efficacy of green practices at Greek ports for maritime energy management. The application of the study is an evolutionary game model that explains the complex interplay of incentives, policies, and strategies within the maritime industry. The observation that the government consistently opts for incentives is that port enterprises lean towards shore power implementation and liner companies that seek to modify shore power facilities. Additionally, the study underscores the significant impact of the government's initial strategy on the evolution of port enterprises and liner companies (Xu et al., 2021). This emphasizes the need for coordinated efforts to align sustainable maritime energy management strategies. Since Greek ports endeavor to enhance their environmental performance and energy management, these findings underscore the importance of government support, policy cost considerations, and social benefits in shaping green practices and shore power technologies within the maritime sector. Hence, it is important to understand the dynamics of stakeholder interactions and strategies for Greek ports that aim to navigate the path towards sustainable and energy-efficient operations. Finally, Iris and Lam (2019) present a systematic literature review that explicates the efficacy of green practices at Greek ports for maritime energy management. Greek ports grapple with the need to enhance energy efficiency and align with evolving environmental regulations regarding innovative technologies and operational strategies. The transition from fossil fuels to low-carbon energy sources like renewable energy and alternative fuels like LNG and hydrogen is substantial for sustainable port operations. Identifying operational strategies such as peak shaving and optimization and adopting electrification, cold-ironing, and energy storage systems offers actionable insights for Greek ports (Iris & Lam, 2019). Moreover, the emphasis on smarter power distribution systems and energy management synchronizes directly with the pursuit of green maritime practices. Therefore, the research gaps are highlighted to untap the opportunities to further enhance energy efficiency, reduce emissions, and contribute significantly to the goals of environmental protection and sustainable energy management in the maritime industry.

Green Shipping Practices

Another key theme of the topic is to know about the green shipping practices that are implemented at ports. According to Prokopenko and Miśkiewicz (2020), the concept of "green shipping" is evolving in the context of the COVID-19 pandemic, highlighting the relevance and need for adaptation. The study's findings are a crucial shift from a sole focus on ecological friendliness to encompass broader aspects of safety and humanity-friendliness within the green shipping paradigm. This shift acknowledges the intricate challenges posed by the pandemic that emphasizes that mere environmental considerations are insufficient for ensuring shipping companies' resilience and financial stability. The research has proposed reevaluating the "green shipping" concept to introduce new instruments to achieve ecological and biological safety in the maritime industry (Prokopenko & Miśkiewicz, 2020). These insights are particularly significant for Greek ports as they grapple with the multifaceted challenges to ensure maritime energy management, environmental sustainability, and biological safety in the wake of the pandemic. So, the study emphasize to revist and update the green shipping concept in response to adverse economic and social conditions to guide international investments and policies for a more resilient and sustainable maritime sector. Another study by Lam and Li (2019) is concerned with the efficacy of green practices at Greek ports to ensure maritime energy management and sustainability. The investigation into the green marketing status of major ports worldwide accentuates the growing importance of sustainability considerations in the maritime industry. The research has recognized that more than half of the 30 major ports are actively engaged in green marketing, which signifies a global trend towards environmentally responsible practices within the maritime industry. This trend aligns with the broader goals to mitigate climate change and conserve energy, which are central to the research question (Lam & Li, 2019). Furthermore, the research emphasizes the need for ports to connect strategies, structures, and functions in their green marketing efforts. It offers practical insights for Greek ports seeking to enhance their environmental performance and competitiveness. Hence, by adopting a holistic approach that balances economic, social, and environmental objectives, Greek ports can attract and retain customers who value sustainability and contribute to the larger goal to achieve maritime energy management and environmental sustainability.

It is also observed by research that green practices are a source of sustainability. According to Rebelo (2020), green shipping directly impacts the research question's focus on the efficacy of green practices at Greek ports. The challenge to secure financing for cleaner and more fuel-efficient technologies is a significant barrier to adopting sustainable maritime practices, including those in Greek ports. The absence of a standardized taxonomy or framework for 'green' maritime activities hampers the ability of financial institutions to channel funds effectively into sustainable shipping projects. Consequently, this gap not only affects shipowners to seek compliance with regulatory requirements but also impedes the broader goal of achieving maritime energy management and environmental sustainability in the Greek maritime industry. So, through advocacy for a globally recognized green-shipping vernacular or classification system, the research has addressed an important issue that can incentivize investors and facilitate the implementation of green practices in Greek ports and the wider maritime sector. A case study of Greek ports by Visvardis (2019) has examined the current state of Greek ports and their efforts towards sustainability and green policies. This study provides valuable insights into the extent to which Greek ports align with international regulations and initiatives that are aimed at preventing environmental pollution and promoting sustainable development. The analysis of actions taken by Greek ports includes prominent examples of 'green ports' that offer practical lessons and inspiration for the maritime industry in Greece. Additionally, the research findings proposed for 'greening' Greek ports can directly contribute to the research question's goal to understand and enhance the maritime industry's environmental sustainability efforts. Therefore, this study serves as a foundational resource to evaluate the efficacy of green practices in Greek ports as it guides future endeavors in maritime energy management and sustainability within the Greek maritime sector.

It is observed that the port of Pireaus and Greek ports, in general, have been working on sustainability for a long time. According to Platias & Spyrou (2023), EU-funded energy-related projects in the Port of Piraeus are empirical evidence of such initiatives' tangible impacts and benefits within the port industry. They showcase how these projects have contributed to achieving energy and environmental objectives and catalyzed sustainability efforts and setting of goals. The research underscores the practical significance of green practices in Greek ports through the identification of positive externalities resulting from project implementation (Platias & Spyrou, 2023). The research highlights the potential ripple effects and broader advantages that such initiatives can bring to the maritime sector. Hence, this study reinforces the importance of green practices and sustainable energy management in Greek ports that sheds light on their potential to drive positive change and enhance the industry's environmental performance to align with the overarching research question. Lastly, the findings of Delis (2022) explained the historical context of steam navigation in Greece, which appears distant from the contemporary research question. The study underscores the vital role maritime innovation and connectivity have played in the country's development. The advent of steam navigation through the Hellenic Steam Navigation Company brought about profound fluctuations in domestic seaborne communications, living standards, and economic, social, and cultural integration. This historical context underscores the transformative power of advancements in maritime technology and infrastructure that accentuates their potential to reshape the transportation landscape and broader socio-economic and cultural aspects (Delis, 2022). In the context of the research question on the efficacy of green practices at Greek ports for maritime energy management, this historical perspective is a reminiscence that innovations in the maritime industry have historically driven significant changes in Greek society and economy. Therefore, the implementation of sustainable practices in modern Greek ports is aligned with contemporary environmental and energy concerns that can lead to transformative outcomes in terms of sustainability and environmental responsibility.

Efficiency of Green Shipping Practices

The efficiency of green shipping practices has been observed over the years, and there are various perspectives in this regard. According to Streimikiene and colleagues (2021), the indicators framework is used to assess low carbon just energy transition, its application in Lithuania and Greece, and the efficacy of green practices at Greek ports for maritime energy management. The study found in the context of low carbon energy transition and its implications for energy poverty and vulnerability at the household level. The research explicates the interconnectedness of environmental, social, and economic dimensions in achieving a sustainable energy development path that aligns with the goals of green practices at ports (Streimikiene et al., 2021). The findings highlight the importance of addressing energy poverty issues while transitioning to renewable energy sources. For the Greek ports, this research suggests that green practices should not only focus on environmental benefits but also consider their social and economic impacts, which contributes to a more holistic and sustainable maritime energy management. Another article by Tsita and colleagues (2020) highlights Greece's current status and potential future directions for biofuel production. It sheds light on a critical aspect of the efforts of the country to decarbonize its transport sector. The study identifies nine next-generation biofuels that range from advanced bioethanol to bio-dimethyl-ether as a potential alternative to conventional fossil fuels. It emphasizes the importance of diversifying fuel sources and integrating biomass processes into biorefineries to produce biofuels and generate valuable byproducts. The research findings underscore the role of biofuels, especially those derived from lignocellulosic biomass and agricultural residues as they help to achieve sustainable and low-carbon energy solutions for sea transport sector pf Greece. This research aligns with broader efforts worldwide to transition towards cleaner and more environmentally friendly energy sources that contributes towards the reduction of greenhouse gas emissions and the promotion of a greener and more sustainable future. To know about this concept more, the idea of circular economy is explored in the context of the maritime industry. According to Dey and colleagues (2022), the adoption of Circular Economy (CE) practices among small and medium-sized enterprises (SMEs) in France, Greece, Spain, and the UK is essential to assess its impact on sustainability performance. The research utilized a mixed-methods approach, including surveys, interviews, and case studies. The study reveals that CE adoption can lead to enhanced environmental performance through increased energy and resource efficiency along with waste reduction. The study identifies the 'design' aspect as the most influential factor in driving CE adoption within SMEs, while the 'recover' component lags behind in current practices. In the maritime sector, this approach allows policymakers to have support and self-motivation to drive CE adoption. Hence, the research proposes an implementation framework for guiding marine industry to develop strategic initiatives for CE adoption across their business operations that could lead to sustainability. The efficiency of these green initiatives is also assessed by Mallouppas and colleagues (2022) as they explored the the key barriers to the widespread adoption of green ammonia as an alternative fuel within the maritime industry. The analysis encompasses various factors that are composed of the technoeconomic challenges, limitations, and supply chain issues associated with ammonia as a maritime fuel. It also considers factors like production costs, geographical availability for bunkering, the need for expanded production capacity, and the development of specific regulations. The research underscores the complexities surrounding ammonia's potential as a zero-carbon maritime fuel by considering its entire lifecycle. Hence, it is vital to address sustainability goals within the industry where policymakers and stakeholders can evaluate ammonia's role to achieve maritime decarbonization objectives. Moreover, the findings of Tzanakakis and colleagues (2020) are focused on water management challenges in Crete, an island in the South Mediterranean Sea. Despite having sufficient water resources under average meteorological conditions, the island faces frequent water scarcity issues especially in the eastern-southern regions. These challenges stem from various factors, including seasonal variations in water availability and demand, over-exploitation of groundwater, low water use efficiencies in agriculture, limited utilization of non-conventional water sources, inadequate monitoring and control frameworks, and insufficient cooperation among stakeholders. These deficiencies not only impact water use efficiency and resource quality but also pose risks to ecosystems along with adaptation to climate variability. In order to address these challenges, the research highlights the need for improved water governance, integrated water management plans, and collaboration among stakeholders. Thus, specific actions need to be applied, including utilizing alternative water sources, implementing efficient water use practices, revising pricing policies, and enhancing monitoring and control mechanisms that can foster research and innovation to support these efforts. Lastly, according to the findings of Kyvelou and Ierapetritis (2020), there exists a significant role of small-scale fisheries in the Mediterranean region where the economic, social, and cultural importance are acknowledged. Despite their substantial impact on coastal communities, these artisanal fisheries often lack adequate data and integration into local development strategies. For this research, Greece is the focal point where the country with vast potential in both fisheries and tourism tends to explore the possibilities to co-develop these sectors (Kyvelou & Ierapetritis, 2020). The examination of the co-existence of artisanal fisheries and tourism where the research has identified the advantages, challenges, and opportunities perceived by various stakeholders that include Fisheries Local Action Groups (FLAGs). In conclusion, sustainable livelihoods in small-scale fisheries depend on synergies between fisheries and other marine activities that offers a "win-win" scenario for sustainable local development and a soft multi-use marine spatial planning approach for coastal communities in economic, environmental, social, cultural, and governance aspects.

Case Studies

There are various case studies of Greece that explain the maritime industry. According to Vagiona (2021), there are various challenges in prioritizing and ranking suitable locations for solar photovoltaic (PV) farms that are focused on the island of Rhodes, Greece. It employs Geographical Information Systems (GIS) for the identification of feasible sites for PV farm deployment and applies four different Multicriteria Decision Making (MCDM) methods for evaluation and ranking. The MCDM methods compared are the Analytical Hierarchy Process (AHP), Technique for Order Preference by Similarity to Ideal Solution (TOPSIS), VIKOR, and PROMETHEE II, where the study reveals that these different MCDM techniques can yield variable rankings for the identified sites. Therefore, the simultaneous use of multiple MCDM methods is recommended for helping decision-makers select the most sustainable PV farm locations that consider each approach's strengths and weaknesses. Another article by Konstantakopoulos and colleagues (2021) focused on the critical issue of city logistics and the last-mile distribution of goods in terms of increasing consumer demands that have led to traffic congestion, noise, and pollution in urban areas. In order to address these challenges and promote green logistics, the research has proposed a sustainable approach where logistics companies collaborate and share their fleets and resources to route and schedule operations. The research has assessed the potential improvements in terms of pollution reduction and cost savings to compare the collaborative approach to the scenario where companies operate independently. Hence, the research draws on real-world data from daily distribution cases handled by Third-Party Logistics companies in Greece to employ a heuristic algorithm for analyzing both individual and collaborative operational strategies.

Another research by Banias and colleagues (2020) has explained addressing the pressing issue of Municipal Solid Waste (MSW) management and its transition towards more sustainable practices in the Region of Central Macedonia (RCM). These managerial aspects are aligned with the European Commission's goals for a circular economy. The research has comprehensively analyzed various MSW treatment methods that are assessed from an environmental perspective. The research gathered data from the Greek National Waste Management Plan. Different scenarios are evaluated, including landfilling with and without energy recovery, recycling, mechanical-biological treatment, composting, anaerobic digestion with energy recovery, and incineration with energy recovery. The findings emphasize the critical role of sorting the waste efficiently in the successful implementation of an integrated waste management system that highlights the importance of sustainable MSW management practices for RCM and beyond. This emphasizes that the land waste is in excess and needs to be managed, and this waste is also associated with increased marine pollution that affects environmental sustainability.

Another study by Kalogiannidis and colleagues (2023) conducted a study in Greece to explore the role of local and regional authorities' role in fostering inclusive, resilient, and green recovery practices where these practices help achieve sustainable development. The research collected data from a survey of 190 leaders from various authorities in West Macedonia that revealed a significant and positive relationship between these recovery strategies and sustainable development. The research has underscored the importance of addressing socioeconomic, climate change, and biodiversity challenges in a coordinated manner rather than in isolation (Kalogiannidis et al., 2023). The research has highlighted the interconnected consequences of these issues, emphasizing the need for a strategic approach to mitigate their impacts. The research findings emphasize the maintenance of existing growth patterns with underlying economic deficiencies and delayed action that leads to increased costs that affect the most vulnerable populations.

Moreover, a case study presented by Leka and others (2022) was conducted in the Mediterranean region, focusing on islands that face challenges. This study has explored the Tourism Carrying Capacity (TCC) approach as a means to assess and monitor tourism development in the coastal areas of the Mediterranean islands. The research has made use of the Pressure-State-Response (PSR) framework for developing a Tourism Carrying Capacity Index (TCCI). The research has emphasized environmental and manmade dimensions while incorporating tourism-specific variables where the TCCI serves as a decision-making tool for assessing and monitoring coastal tourism sustainability. The case has demonstrated the ideology of Naxos, Greece. Hence, this approach provides valuable insights to plan more sustainable tourism pathways in coastal areas and offers potential for replication in terms of implementation.

Finally, the case study of the Danube presented by Mako and colleagues (2021) is focused on assessing the sustainability of transport systems, especially the examination of the potential of using navigable waterways like the Danube as an effective solution to reduce road and railway transport to promote sustainability. The research has developed a model to reveal the available capacity of the Danube waterway to compare it with real transport performance data. The connection of this model to the production of fossil fuels serves as a case study that has presented the demonstration of the possibility of transitioning from road transport to inland water transport in a sustainable and environmentally friendly manner for specific transport routes. Therefore, this research is an application of sustainable capacity utilization models for encouraging the shift towards environmentally friendly inland water transport, which shows that the Danube's available capacity could support this transition. This case study is a subset of the issue, which explains that it is pertinent to solve the issue of pollution in all spheres of life to ensure that the green economy is sustained.

Research Gap

The literature review provides a comprehensive overview of research on the efficacy of green practices at Greek ports for maritime energy management, focusing on various themes and case studies. The review has covered aspects like maritime energy management, green shipping practices, the efficiency of these practices, and specific case studies conducted in Greece. The research in the context of maritime energy management has highlighted the importance of collaboration, communication, knowledge sharing, and human capital to implement green practices effectively at Greek ports. The research emphasizes the significance of decision-making processes and adherence to international standards to optimize energy management strategies that include shore power and LNG bunkering. Regarding green shipping practices, the review has discussed the evolving concept of green shipping, its relevance during the COVID-19 pandemic, and the need for considering broader aspects of safety and humanity-friendliness within this paradigm. Moreover, the research also explicated the role of green marketing at major ports worldwide along with the potential to attract sustainability-conscious customers while meeting environmental goals. So, the review has addressed the efficiency of green shipping practices that focus on indicators for low-carbon energy transition, biofuel production, circular economy adoption, and the use of ammonia as an alternative fuel within the maritime industry. So, the research articles have emphasized the interconnectedness of environmental, social, and economic dimensions and advocate for a holistic approach to sustainability. Furthermore, several case studies in the Greek context provide insights into waste management, water scarcity, small-scale fisheries, and local and regional authorities' role in sustainable development. These cases demonstrate the practical challenges and opportunities to implement green practices for achieving maritime energy management and environmental sustainability. However, despite the extensive coverage of relevant research, the review has pointed out a gap related to the intent of the efficacy of green practices at Greek ports, specifically to prevent the excessive use of shore power and promote the increased use of LNG. This gap suggests further research to investigate and address these specific aspects of maritime energy management at Greek ports. Hence, the review has provided a key foundation for the research, but it has highlighted the gap that is effectively mitigated through the conduction of primary research in the next section.

Summary and Transition

This chapter is the most comprehensive one as it explains the key themes of literature by studying the background through a historical perspective along with understanding theoretical and conceptual frameworks. Then, the literature review is conducted where maritime energy management, green shipping practices, efficiency of green shipping practices, and case studies are expounded. Now, the literature is established, and the key motivation to conduct this research is derived. So, the next chapter is focused on the research methodology, design, intervention, and data analysis plans discretely.

Chapter 3

Research Method

The literature review has offered a comprehensive exploration of various aspects related to the efficacy of green practices at Greek ports for maritime energy management. The secondary research has covered themes that include maritime energy management, green shipping practices, the efficiency of these practices, and specific case studies per the Greek context. Throughout the review, it becomes evident that there is a notable gap related to the effectiveness of green practices to curb excessive shore power usage and promote increased adoption of LNG (Liquefied Natural Gas) at Greek ports. Based on the insights garnered from the literature, the primary research is conducted in quantitative form to assess the research question. It is important to conduct primary research as it adds value to the research while making it valid and credible (Lê & Schmid, 2022). Moreover, keeping the literature review intact, the following is the restated research question.

RQ: To what extent do green practices implemented at Greek ports effectively reduce excessive shore power usage and promote the increased adoption of LNG for maritime energy management?

The restated hypotheses are:

H00: There is no significant impact of green practices implemented at Greek ports due to effective shore power usage and the promotion of increased adoption of LNG for maritime energy management.

H01: There is a significant impact of green practices implemented at Greek ports due to effective shore power usage and the promotion of increased adoption of LNG for maritime energy management.

This research question and hypotheses directly address the literature gap and serve as the focal point for the upcoming methodology, data collection, analysis, and findings. It seeks to provide a deeper understanding of how Greek ports are currently implementing green practices and their impact on energy management in achieving the intended goals related to shore power reduction and LNG adoption.

Research Design and Rationale

The research design for this particular thesis question is quantitative research through a survey where a questionnaire is prepared to get answers in the form of ratings (Asmus & Radocy, 2012; Harrell & Harrell, 2015). Then, the survey data is quantitatively analyzed through t-tests and ANOVA variance test, where the descriptive statistics are also done to understand the efficacy of green practices at Greek ports for maritime energy management (Babii, 2020). Quantitative research is particularly well-suited for addressing the research question and objectives that are outlined in the study. The use of a quantitative framework is to assess the extent to which green practices reduce shore power usage and promote LNG adoption. The quantitative methods allow for the precise measurement of variables related to these objectives where, through surveys, numerical data is collected (Sileyew, 2019). The data is quantified in the current state of green practices and energy management at Greek ports. The second reason to select this framework is objectivity and the use of structured data collection methods where surveys provide standardized questions and response options. This helps to minimize bias and ensure that responses are not influenced by the researcher's interpretation (Leichsenring et al.,

2017). This objectivity enhances the reliability of the study while allowing for the generalizability of findings to a larger population of Greek ports and beyond. The third aspect of this analysis is the variable answers for green practices at Greek ports, where the quantitative approach allows for collecting data from a relatively large sample of Greek ports, increasing the study's representativeness (Egbert et al., 2022). This is particularly valuable to investigate practices across different ports and assess their impact. Moreover, the research has statistical significance where t-tests and ANOVA variance tests are powerful statistical tools to analyze and draw meaningful conclusions from survey data (Becker et al., 2016). They help to determine whether observed differences in green practices and energy management are statistically significant or are generated merely due to chance. Furtheremore, the research is an opportunity to compare means between two groups i.e., ports with and without specific green practices through t-test. This enables identification of significant differences in energy management outcomes. In contrast, ANOVA variance tests extend this analysis to compare means across more than two groups that allows for a comprehensive examination of various green practices. Another reason to conduct the research is the fact that Greek ports and stakeholders often require data-driven insights to make informed decisions about the adoption of green practices. This insight is provided through quantitative research that can guide port authorities, shipping companies, and policymakers in optimizing their energy management strategies. Additionally, this design is scalable, which makes it feasible to collect data from multiple ports efficiently. Moreover, it is replicable and allows other researchers to apply similar methods to different geographic regions or industries for comparative analysis. The research question also involves an assessment of the effectiveness of green practices in terms of numerical outcomes like reductions in shore power usage and increases in LNG adoption. So, the quantitative research methods are tailored to capture and analyze numerical data, making them befitting for this purpose. The statistical tests used are also helpful in testing the hypothesis as specific relations can be formulated through the structured approach, allowing for hypothesis confirmation or rejection based on empirical data. The quantitative answers also sets basis for policy implications in the Greek maritime industry and environmental regulations. Moreover, the surveys are designed effectively that provides an efficient way to collect data from a large number of respondents where this approach can save time and resources compared to qualitative methods like interviews or observations. Lastly, apart from measurement of the efficacy of green practices, quantitative research can help quantify challenges and opportunities associated with their implementation. Hence, the selection of a quantitative research design with surveys, t-tests, and ANOVA variance tests is rooted in the need for precise measurement, objectivity, generalizability, and statistical rigor where this approach allows for the collection and analysis of data that can answer the research question effectively.

Methodology

The methodology is already explained in the research design. Now to begin actual research, there is a need to make a primary research questionnaire first. The research questionnaire for this study is shown in Appendix B. However, before actually sharing the questionnaire, there is a need to gain consent from the 30 research participants. Since the research participants are specific people who belong to the maritime industry of Greece, these thirty participants are shipmen and managers at the ports. It is essential to get informed consent from them while ensuring that confidentiality is maintained so that their name or personal details are not discussed in research results (Bhandari, 2021; Shah et al., 2022). Appendix A is the research consent form that is shared with the potential participants.

Population

The first aspect to be assessed is the population selected. For this research study, the population consists of shipmen and managers who work at Greek ports. The goal is the selection of a sample of 30 participants from this population with a confidence interval of 95%. The population includes individuals who are directly involved in maritime operations, decision-making, and management within the port facilities. To select a sample, there is a need to estimate the total population size. This can be challenging as it may vary over time due to the dynamic nature of the maritime industry, but it is estimated that among the hundreds of shipmen and managers, only 30 are scrutinized. Though the sample size is relatively smaller to the total number of people. However, for research, the sample size is sufficient for a confidence interval of 95% where a margin of error of ±5% can exist. So, the calculation sample size of the population is 30. The sampling of this population is explained in the following section, where random sampling is employed to ensure that the data is selected per the collection without any bias while stating it.

Sampling and Sampling Procedures

This research aims to evaluate the impact of green practices on shore power usage along with the promotion of LNG adoption at Greek ports. For this purpose, the sampling method selected is convenience sampling. Convenience sampling is suitable for this research due to several practical considerations and the target population's nature (Stratton, 2021). Convenience sampling is a non-probability sampling method that researchers use to select participants based on their ease of access and availability (Sedgwick, 2013). It is a practical approach often used in research to obtain a random or representative sample from a larger population, which is challenging or impractical (Sarker & AL-Muaalemi, 2022). Greek ports have dynamic work environments, with shipmen and managers often engaged in demanding and time-sensitive operations. Therefore, obtaining a truly random or stratified sample from this population can be challenging and lead to low response rates and delays that could compromise the feasibility and timeliness of study. Moreover, convenience sampling offers advantages in terms of accessibility and convenience for data collection, that makes it well-suited for this research. It allows for the selection of participants based on their availability and willingness to participate, which is aligned with the practical constraints of the maritime industry. Additionally, convenience sampling can be cost-effective and efficient, facilitating data gathering from shipmen and managers who can have limited time to engage in lengthy surveys or interview processes. At the same time, it is acknowledged that convenience sampling can introduce some degree of sampling bias (Pickering & Blaszczynski, 2021). So, the primary focus of this research is to gather insights and understand trends rather than to generalize findings for the entire population of shipmen and managers at Greek ports. The research circumscribes to explore perceptions, behaviors, and attitudes within this specific group, where convenience sampling provides a pragmatic approach to achieve this goal. Through appropriate statistical analyses allows that the research can still draw meaningful conclusions and insights regarding the impact of green practices on maritime energy management in Greek ports. Thus, it helps in leveraging the data collected from the accessible and willing participants within the convenience sample. The convenience sampling is directly applied to the data as the findings from questionnaire section where section 1 and section 7 have gained the sample findings. These findings are presented in the form of tables where each participants' answer is stated to apply data analysis effectively.

| Participant No | Section 1 | | |
	Q1	Q2 (Years)	Q3
1	Shipman	10	Patras
2	Manager	2	Piraeus
3	Shipman	4	Corfu
4	Shipman	5	Rafina
5	Shipman	6	Volos
6	Manager	7	Piraeus
7	Shipman	2	Volos
8	Manager	1	Patras
9	Shipman	4	Rafina
10	Manager	6	Piraeus
11	Manager	7	Volos
12	Shipman	8	Corfu
13	Manager	8	Patras
14	Shipman	9	Volos
15	Shipman	6	Piraeus
16	Manager	1	Rafina
17	Shipman	11	Corfu
18	Manager	3	Volos
19	Manager	1	Patras
20	Shipman	7	Piraeus
21	Manager	1.5	Rafina
22	Shipman	9	Patras
23	Shipman	10	Piraeus
24	Manager	1	Volos
25	Shipman	12	Corfu
26	Shipman	9	Patras
27	Shipman	8	Rafina
28	Manager	2	Corfu
29	Shipman	5	Corfu
30	Manager	7	Rafina

Table 3 Population of the Research

The following is the demographic data of the study, which was an optional part, yet it was completed and helped in knowing about the credibility of the sample even more as assessed per the descriptive analysis.

| Participant No | Section 7 | | |
	Gender	Age	Level of education
1	Male	36	High_School
2	Male	28	Bachelors
3	Male	22	High_School
4	Male	23	High_School

5	Male	23	High_School
6	Male	25	Bachelors
7	Male	20	High_School
8	Male	28	Masters
9	Male	23	High_School
10	Male	26	Bachelors
11	Male	37	Masters
12	Male	28	High_School
13	Male	38	Masters
14	Male	29	High_School
15	Male	26	High_School
16	Male	23	Bachelors
17	Male	35	High_School
18	Male	21	Bachelors
19	Male	23	Bachelors
20	Male	33	High_School
21	Male	22	Bachelors
22	Male	29	High_School
23	Male	34	High_School
24	Male	24	Bachelors
25	Male	41	High_School
26	Male	34	High_School
27	Male	36	High_School
28	Female	27	Masters
29	Male	35	High_School
30	Female	38	Masters

Table 4 Demographic Data from Survey

These are the basic aspects of the study that are assessed in the form of descriptive statistics in the data analysis section. This helps in knowing about the data characteristics in a statistical manner (Kaur et al., 2018).

Procedures for Recruitment, Participation, and Data Collection (Primary Data)

The research process involves several systematic steps to effectively investigate the research question and test the hypotheses. The first is the key aspect of ethical considerations that are kept intact through obtaining informed consent from the 30 participants, shipmen, and managers at Greek ports (Holian & Coghlan, 2013). A comprehensive consent form is developed (see Appendix A) that clearly outlines the research's purpose, scope, and expectations. This aspect has ensured that participants understand the voluntary nature of their involvement, the potential risks and benefits, and the confidentiality of their responses. The participants have provided their informed written consent to demonstrate their willingness to participate in the study. Secondly, the participants' recruitment in the research is given specialized attention where the population is appropriately selected, and then the data is collected from 30 participants for convenience sampling. This is an appropriate method as it allows the selection of participants based on their accessibility and willingness to participate. Moreover, it helps in the identification of potential participants through port authorities, industry associations, or direct contact. Once the participants are identified, and consent is obtained, then there is a need to proceed to data collection. For this purpose, a structured questionnaire is designed to capture relevant information (see Appendix B) related to green practices, shore power usage, and LNG adoption at Greek ports (Roopa & Rani, 2012). The survey questions were carefully crafted to align with the variables intended for analysis later by using t-tests and ANOVA variance tests. In order to make sure that appropriate answers were received, the questionnaire was prepared in a clear, concise, and comprehensible manner. Then, the survey was administered electronically to the participants for ease, and the answers were received within the deadline (Ball, 2019). Following data collection, entering and managing the gathered information was necessary. Then, the data is organized in the form of a spreadsheet for checking accuracy and errors in the data while sorting it. Then, the data is embedded in the statistical software for the final data analysis stage. SPSS was used in this regard to perform a comprehensive analysis of the collected data (Okagbue et al., 2021). First, descriptive statistics were used to summarize and visualize the key findings, where this step provides an overview of the data's central tendencies and variations. Then, t-tests are applied to assess whether there is a significant difference between groups or conditions in relation to key variables. In this case, the impact of green practices on shore power usage and LNG adoption is compared by testing the null hypothesis (H00) against the alternative hypothesis (H01). Furthermore, ANOVA variance tests are applied to investigate potential differences between multiple groups, which will help determine whether green practice variations significantly affect LNG adoption for maritime energy management among different categories or sectors within the Greek ports. Hence, the research process systematically guides the study from participant consent and recruitment to data collection and rigorous statistical analysis.

Intervention

Firstly, a survey questionnaire was shared among the participants, where the data was gathered through this intervention. Then, t-tests and ANOVA (Analysis of Variance) are essential statistical tools that are utilized to analyze the relationships between variables in research studies. In the context of this research question, the aim is to examine the impact of green practices on shore power usage and LNG adoption at Greek ports. These statistical tests are eminent for evaluating the hypotheses and assessing the significance of any observed effects. Firstly, a t-test is applied, a statistical hypothesis test used to determine whether a significant difference exists between the means of the two groups. It is employed when a categorical independent variable, i.e., the presence or absence of green practices at Greek ports (section 2), and two continuous dependent variables, i.e., shore power usage (section 3) and LNG adoption (section 4). For this research, the two groups are compared, i.e., group 1 is ports with implemented green practices, and group 2 is ports without implemented green practices. For each group, the data is collected on shore power usage and LNG adoption. The t-test is applied to assess whether the two groups have a statistically significant difference in shore power usage and LNG adoption (Gerald, 2018). If the p-value, i.e., a measure of statistical significance, is below a predetermined threshold, i.e., 0.05 (Mishra et al., 2019). In this case, the null hypothesis (H00) is rejected and concludes that green practices significantly impact these variables. In contrast, ANOVA is used when there are more than two groups to compare (Kim, 2014). It assesses whether there are statistically significant differences among the means of three or more groups where, in this research, ANOVA is used to explore the impact of green practices on shore power usage and LNG adoption across different categories or sectors within Greek ports. The three categories that are made for this research are ports with strong green practices, ports with moderate green practices, and ports with limited green practices (refer to section 5 of Appendix B). In this case, each category represents a group that helps to determine if there are any significant differences in shore power usage and LNG adoption among these categories. Lastly, the practice of ANOVA helps to affirm the statistical findings inferred from the t-test. Similarly to t-test, ANOVA calculates a p-value where if the p-value is below your chosen significance level, i.e., 0.05, then it could be concluded that there are significant differences in shore power usage and LNG adoption across the categories of ports with different levels of green practices. In conclusion, t-tests and ANOVA are powerful tools to assess the impact of green practices, i.e., independent variable on shore power usage and LNG adoption, i.e., dependent variables at Greek ports.

Instrumentation and Operationalization of Constructs

The instrumentation and operationalization of constructs are important aspects of research, as they involve the definition and measurement of the variables of interest in a clear and systematic manner. For this research, the primary constructs of interest are "green practices". "shore power usage", and "LNG adoption" at Greek ports. The constructs that are instrumentalized and operationalized are explained in this section. The first factor is green practices, where the instrumentation refers to the environmentally friendly initiatives and actions implemented at Greek ports. In order to measure this construct, a set of observable indicators and criteria are used to assess the presence and extent of green practices. In contrast, green practices are operationalized to create a checklist or scale that evaluates specific activities and policies. This could include items like the use of renewable energy sources, waste management practices, emissions reduction initiatives, and adherence to environmental regulations. Each item on the checklist can be rated or scored for quantifying the level of green practices at each port, as in section 6. The second factor is shore power usage. This instrument pertains to the extent to which vessels at Greek ports connect to onshore electrical power sources to reduce emissions and fuel consumption while docked. This factor can be operationalized through a collection of data on the frequency and duration of shore power connections for each vessel at the port. This data can be gathered through port records, energy consumption meters, or self-reporting by port authorities, where the operational definition involves quantifying the percentage of time each vessel uses shore power while in port. The third factor is LNG adoption, which refers to the extent to which liquefied natural gas is used as a clean energy source for maritime activities at Greek ports. This factor can be operationalized by collecting data on the number of vessels using LNG as a fuel source, the volume of LNG consumed, and any infrastructure investments related to LNG storage and distribution at the port. For this purpose, a scale can be used to measure the level of LNG adoption, with higher scores indicating greater adoption. So, these constructs are quantified and measured by the use of the described operationalizations where the data is collected through the questionnaire (see appendix B). The information is used to assess the presence and extent of green practices, shore power usage, and LNG adoption at Greek ports. Therefore, these constructs significantly impact each other and align with research questions and hypotheses as the instrumentation and operationalization of constructs ensure that the study is rigorous and that variables are consistent.

Intervention Applications that Involve the Manipulation of an Independent Variable

Intervention applications involve the manipulation of an independent variable and the measurement of dependent variables, which are a fundamental aspect of experimental research. This allows researchers to investigate causal relationships and test hypotheses. For this particular research, the impact of green practices at Greek ports, the independent variable is the level of green practices implemented at the ports, and the dependent variables are shore power usage and LNG adoption. In order to conduct this intervention, there is a need to begin by categorizing the Greek ports into different groups based on the level of green practices they have implemented, like "high green practices," "moderate green practices," and "limited green practices". Secondly, there is a need to manipulate the independent variable to implement interventions or changes in green practices at select ports where it is important to keep others as control groups with their existing green practices intact. In this regard, a few recommendations based on a series of sustainability initiatives are provided that include the installation of renewable energy sources, waste reduction programs, and incentives for LNG adoption, as these practices are categorized as "high green practices". In contrast, ports with "limited green practices" category are the ones who continue with their existing practices such that this manipulation creates distinct groups or conditions within the study. For the manipulation of variables, there is also a need to consider dependent variables. For shore power usage, before conducting the primary research, baseline data is collected from the literature review that serves as a reference and helps in comparing with the primary results. Once the intervention is applied, the research results can be formulated and explained in the form of inference. The second dependent variable is LNG adoption, and similar aspects are implemented for it to know about the key ideas and recommendations for LNG adoption. Once the data is collected, there is a need to apply statistical analyses i.e., t-tests and ANOVA, to assess whether there are statistically significant differences in shore power usage and LNG adoption between the groups with varying levels of green practices. Therefore, intervention applications include manipulating an independent variable, i.e., green practices, and measuring dependent variables, i.e., shore power usage and LNG adoption, designed to provide empirical evidence of the causal relationships hypothesized in this research question and hypotheses. Hence, the experimental approach enables the researcher to conclude the effectiveness of green practices in reducing excessive shore power usage and promoting LNG adoption at Greek ports with higher confidence.

Data Analysis Plan

A data analysis plan is an essential component of any research study, especially in conducting quantitative analysis by the use of statistical tests such as t-tests and ANOVA variance tests. This plan outlines the step-by-step procedures and strategies to analyze the data collected during this research. In this case, the purpose is to assess the impact of green practices on shore power usage and LNG adoption at Greek ports by employing t-tests and ANOVA as they are the primary quantitative analysis tools. The first step of data analysis is data preparation, where the data is kept clean, accurate, and well-organized by checking for any missing values, outliers, or inconsistencies. It is assumed that there are different levels of green practices for every categorical variable. This helped to create a dataset that includes variables for green practices, shore power usage, and LNG adoption at Greek ports. The second step is descriptive statistics to begin the analysis through calculation of each variable as a mean, median, standard deviation, and range. The summary tables and graphs are generated to visualize the central tendencies and variations in the data that provide an overview of the dataset. In the next step, initiate the t-tests for comparing two groups for each pair of groups based on green practices. Then, the hypothesis is tested through the value of significance by recording p-values. If the p-value is less than the chosen significance level, then the null hypothesis is rejected to conclude that there is a significant difference. After the t-test, the ANOVA variance test is applied to compare multiple groups, i.e., high, moderate, and limited green practices. The hypothesis is tested such that if the results show a significant difference, then the hypothesis is accepted. The ANOVA variance and t-test are interpreted in the next step to consider the p-values and their impact. This helps provide a clear and concise summary of the findings, implications, and practical significance aligned with the existing literature on green practices in maritime energy management at Greek ports. So, this is the data analysis plan where different limitations exist, like the specific sample size, data collected constraints, and lack of future assessment. Hence, following this data analysis plan, there is a need to systematically analyze the data and determine whether green practices' significant impact on shore power usage and LNG adoption at Greek ports provide valuable insights into maritime energy management practices.

Threats to Validity

There are three types of threats to the validity of quantitative research: external, internal, and construct. Apart from these threats, the ethical considerations are assessed in the following section. Each of the threats from the perspective of the research is discussed below.

External Validity

External validity is the extent to which the findings of a research study can be generalized to other populations, settings, and conditions beyond the specific sample in the context of this research. While assessing the impact of green practices at Greek ports on shore power usage and LNG adoption, there are several threats to external validity should be considered. One significant threat to external validity is the potential bias in selecting participants, i.e., sampling bias (Hughes et al., 2021). This study focuses on shipmen and managers at Greek ports, which do not fully represent the entire population of maritime professionals or other geographic regions. If the chosen participants do not adequately reflect the diversity and characteristics of the broader population, then it limits the generalizability of the research findings to the wider maritime industry (Delios et al., 2022). The second external threat is setting validity, where different Greek ports are chosen for assessment while other regions are ignored. This could limit the external validity of the research findings as the impact of green practices on shore power usage and LNG adoption can vary significantly in different maritime settings worldwide. The third external validity is temporal validity where the effectiveness of green practices to reduce shore power usage and promote LNG adoption that can change over time due to evolved technologies, policies, and market dynamics. These study findings are relevant only to the specific time frame in which data, which was collected and cannot be applied to future or past periods. Another threat is of measurement validity, where the measurements and the accuracy of the instruments used in data collection are essential for external validity. This implies that if the data collected from the survey is not appropriately designed or validated, then the reliability and generalizability of the findings can be compromised. Additionally, there is a threat to validity in terms of the Hawthorne effect, which is the awareness regarding the influence of the study where shipmen and managers at Greek ports can alter their practices or responses due to this awareness that leads to results that do not accurately reflect their typical behaviors in a non-research setting. Furthermore, Greece's cultural, economic, and regulatory context can significantly differ from other countries and regions, impacting the applicability of the findings to a global or cross-cultural context. Lastly, there can exist selection bias in the process of selecting ports at various levels of green practices (Smith, 2020). This means that the sample of ports might not accurately represent the broader population of ports in Greece or other maritime regions. Hence, to enhance the external validity of the research, there is a need to address these threats by careful justification of the sample selection that provides a clear description of the study setting in the context of the Greek maritime industry and beyond.

Internal Validity

Internal validity is the extent to which a research study accurately establishes a causal relationship between the independent variable i.e., green practices at Greek ports, and the dependent variables i.e., shore power usage and LNG adoption, while ruling out alternative explanations. There are several threats to internal validity, the first one is the changes that occur during the study period, unrelated to green practices that can affect shore power usage and LNG adoption (Holmes, 2020). The second one is that the perceptions of the same participants may change with time as they mature and it is a natural phenomenon that cannot be avoided. The testing effect can also exist where the measurement of shore power usage and LNG adoption through surveys can sensitize participants to the research objectives that cause them to alter their behaviors or responses. There is also a chance of inconsistencies in the measurement instruments, like the use of surveys, which can affect the reliability and validity of research results. There is also a chance of statistical artifacts that can affect the overall results. Moreover, in the selection of green practices, inherent differences can exist that can affect the outcomes. Furthermore, suppose the participants in the control group perceive themselves as disadvantaged by not receiving the green practices intervention. In that case, it can consciously or unconsciously change their behaviors, which can distort the results. Another internal threat is that historical events can influence green practices that affect shore power usage and LNG adoption. Lastly, in case of industry-wide policy changes or technological breakthroughs, shore power usage and LNG adoption can impact it, making it difficult to isolate the effects of green practices. In order to mitigate these threats to internal validity, there is a need to consider the use of control groups, random assignment, and pre-post measurements along with thorough documentation.

Construct Validity

Construct validity is concerned with the extent to which the chosen measures accurately represent the underlying theoretical constructs in the research, specifically the concepts of green practices, shore power usage, and LNG adoption at Greek ports. There are several threats associated with construct validity. If the survey questions are not carefully designed or validated, the assessment may not be accurately captured, leading to measurement error and reduced construct validity. There is also a mono-operation bias that could be handled by using various data sources to add credibility to the research findings. Moreover, participants can respond in ways that make their behaviors or practices appear more socially desirable, which can distort the true representation of green practices, shore power usage, and LNG adoption. There can also exist compound effects, e.g., shore power usage can be influenced by both green practices and economic factors that complicate the assessment of the unique impact of green practices. Moreover, over time, the meaning of the findings is bound to change due to transition in the practices at ports. Lastly, certain expectations about the effects of green practices can exist, which can inadvertently influence data collection or interpretation that potentially leads to biased results. Hence, to enhance construct validity, refined questions are established and validated to measure scales when available and employ multiple measures to assess the same constructs from different angles.

Ethical Procedures

In this research, rigorous ethical procedures were applied to ensure the rights and well-being of the shipmen and managers at Greek ports participants. The ethical considerations included getting informed consent from all participants, which involved providing clear and comprehensive consent forms that outline the research's purpose, scope, potential risks, and benefits (Holian & Coghlan, 2013). Participants were assured of the confidentiality of their responses since the recruitment process prioritized participant autonomy and voluntariness. Moreover, convenience sampling was employed to respect participants' accessibility and willingness to participate. The data collection process was conducted with utmost transparency; the participants were allowed to withdraw at any stage. Additionally, all data were securely stored and anonymized to protect participants' privacy. The research adhered to ethical guidelines and standards, which ensured that it was conducted ethically and responsibly and upheld the principles of integrity, respect, and confidentiality throughout the research process.

Summary

So, this chapter has laid out the methodology of the research, where it is explained that the t-test and ANOVA variance test is applied. This chapter has explained the steps taken for this research along with the threats associated with the research application. So, it has the basiss for data analysis. In the next chapter, the results are presented. Firstly, the independent variables data is collected, followed by the t-test and ANOVA variance test and their respective results. This is the most important aspect of primary analysis that helps infer the research question.

Chapter 4

Results

The chapter presents data in tabular form along with its results and coded form of data with numeric details followed by statistical results and graphs based on descriptive statistics. It investigates the research question from a statistical point of view. The data collection is done in this chapter, followed by the application of the t-test and ANOVA variance test.

Data Collection

The collected data from the survey is presented here. The data from sections 1 and 7 was about demographic properties, so it was stated in the population section. However, the analysis of the demographics is presented in the study results of this chapter. Now, the rest of the sections are presented here based on the scrutiny of which test is applied to a particular section. The data collected for the t-test is as follows:

The key for the data collected is that 0=No, 1=Yes, 2=Not sure

Participant No.	Independent Variable Section 2		Dependent Variables					
			Section 3			Section 4		
	Q1	Q2	Q1	Q2	Q3	Q1	Q2	Q3
1	0		2			1	20%	
2	0		2			0		Maintenance problems
3	0		1	45%		0		Leakage issues
4	0		2			2		
5	0		2			2		
6	0		0		Cost increase	2		
7	0		2			1	20%	
8	0		2			0		Maintenance problems
9	0		2			2		
10	0		1	30%		2		
11	0		0		Reduced shipping rate	1	20%	
12	1	Use of LNG	2			2		
13	0		2			0		Leakage
14	0		2			2		
15	0		2			2		
16	1	Shore power	1	30%		2		
17	0		1	25%		2		

18	0		0		Increased cost	0		Maintenance issues
19	0		2			2		
20	0		2			1	25%	
21	0		2			0		Leakage issues
22	1	Specific times for ships to move	1	45%		2		
23	0		2			2		
24	0		2			2		
25	0		2			2		
26	0		0		Increased cost	1	20%	
27	1	Use of LNG fuel	1	25%		2		
28	0		2			2		
29	0		2			0		Maintenance issues
30	1	Use of LNG fuel	2			2		

Table 4 Data for T-test Analysis

For the application of ANOVA variance test section 5 is considered where level of agreement or disagreement of participants is analyzed on a scale of 1 to 5. Here, 1 = Strongly Disagree; 2 = Disagree; 3 = Neutral; 4 = Agree; 5 = Strongly Agree

Participant No.	Section 5	
	Group 1 (Q1)	Group 2 (Q2)
1	4	3
2	2	4
3	3	4
4	4	5
5	4	2
6	3	3
7	2	2
8	3	3
9	3	2
10	4	3
11	4	4
12	2	3
13	3	3
14	4	4
15	1	3

16	2	2
17	2	2
18	3	4
19	4	3
20	3	4
21	4	3
22	2	2
23	3	4
24	3	4
25	3	4
26	4	3
27	4	3
28	2	4
29	3	4
30	3	3

Table 5 Data for ANOVA analysis

Finally, the last section of the survey is to get a qualitative idea of the overall research question, and it was kept optional so that only those who wanted to get involved in it. It was noted that most of the participants ignored it, and only two participants answered it. One participant said that green practices must be ensured for the sustainability of the environment. In contrast, the other participant said that marine life must be protected and pollution must be catered to through effective green practices for maintaining a positive impact on the marine system.

Treatment and/or Intervention Fidelity

In order to treat all this data, the first step is to use the population data from the sampling section and apply descriptive statistical analysis to know about the participants and their involvement in the research. Once the descriptive statistics and bar charts are explicated, the t-test is conducted to test the impact of the independent variable on the dependent variable while testing for the hypothesis. Once the answer to the t-test is received, the ANOVA variance test is applied to affirm the results. In this case, the two groups that are presented in the data table are used in the SPSS to assess per the ANOVA method, and the hypothesis is then tested. Lastly, keeping the secondary findings from the literature review and primary findings from the t-test and ANOVA test, the research results are presented. All these aspects also helped in knowing about a descriptive aspect of the research in clearer terms while answering the research question.

Study Results

Descriptive Statistics

The measures of central tendency and different aspects of descriptive analysis were calculated in SPSS in the form of a table followed by bar charts. The descriptive statistics of the sample are as follows:

Statistics							
		Job role	Years of experience	Name of port	Gender	Age	Level of education
N	Valid	30	30	30	30	30	30
	Missing	0	0	0	0	0	0
Mean			5.7500			28.9000	
Median			6.0000			28.0000	
Mode			1.00a			23.00	
Std. Deviation			3.32895			6.14396	
Variance			11.082			37.748	
Range			11.00			21.00	
Sum			172.50			867.00	
a. Multiple modes exist. The smallest value is shown							

Table 6 Overall Descriptives of Sample

Now, the frequency tables are also made on SPSS. It suggests that 43.3% of the sample was composed of managers, while 56.7% were shipmen. Moreover, 13.3% of people had experience of 1 and 7 years, 3.3% had experience of 1.5, 11, and 12 years, 10% had 2,6,8, and 9 years, 6.5% had 4,5 and 10 years. It was also found that 20% of the sample worked at Corfu, 20% at Piraeus, 20% at Patras, 20% at Rafina, and 20% at Volos. The sample had only 6.7% females, while 93.3% were males. They all belong to various ages, where most of them had a high school diploma (56.7%), while only 26.7% had a bachelor's and 16.7% had a master's degree. These are the descriptive statistics of the sample that were used in deriving the t-test and ANOVA test results.

Job Role		Frequency	Percent	Valid Percent	Cumulative Percent
Valid	Manager	13	43.3	43.3	43.3
	Shipman	17	56.7	56.7	100.0
	Total	30	100.0	100.0	

Years of experience		Frequency	Percent	Valid Percent	Cumulative Percent
Valid	1.00	4	13.3	13.3	13.3
	1.50	1	3.3	3.3	16.7
	2.00	3	10.0	10.0	26.7
	3.00	1	3.3	3.3	30.0
	4.00	2	6.7	6.7	36.7
	5.00	2	6.7	6.7	43.3
	6.00	3	10.0	10.0	53.3
	7.00	4	13.3	13.3	66.7
	8.00	3	10.0	10.0	76.7
	9.00	3	10.0	10.0	86.7
	10.00	2	6.7	6.7	93.3
	11.00	1	3.3	3.3	96.7
	12.00	1	3.3	3.3	100.0

		Frequency	Percent	Valid Percent	Cumulative Percent
	Total	30	100.0	100.0	

Name of port					
		Frequency	Percent	Valid Percent	Cumulative Percent
Valid	Corfu	6	20.0	20.0	20.0
	Patras	6	20.0	20.0	40.0
	Piraeus	6	20.0	20.0	60.0
	Rafina	6	20.0	20.0	80.0
	Volos	6	20.0	20.0	100.0
	Total	30	100.0	100.0	

Gender					
		Frequency	Percent	Valid Percent	Cumulative Percent
Valid	Female	2	6.7	6.7	6.7
	Male	28	93.3	93.3	100.0
	Total	30	100.0	100.0	

Age					
		Frequency	Percent	Valid Percent	Cumulative Percent
Valid	20.00	1	3.3	3.3	3.3
	21.00	1	3.3	3.3	6.7
	22.00	2	6.7	6.7	13.3
	23.00	5	16.7	16.7	30.0
	24.00	1	3.3	3.3	33.3
	25.00	1	3.3	3.3	36.7
	26.00	2	6.7	6.7	43.3
	27.00	1	3.3	3.3	46.7
	28.00	3	10.0	10.0	56.7
	29.00	2	6.7	6.7	63.3
	33.00	1	3.3	3.3	66.7
	34.00	2	6.7	6.7	73.3
	35.00	2	6.7	6.7	80.0
	36.00	2	6.7	6.7	86.7
	37.00	1	3.3	3.3	90.0
	38.00	2	6.7	6.7	96.7
	41.00	1	3.3	3.3	100.0
	Total	30	100.0	100.0	

Level of Education					
		Frequency	Percent	Valid Percent	Cumulative Percent
Valid	Bachelors	8	26.7	26.7	26.7
	High_School	17	56.7	56.7	83.3
	Masters	5	16.7	16.7	100.0
	Total	30	100.0	100.0	

Table 7 Frequency of the Descriptive Data

The bar charts of the descriptive statistics are presented.

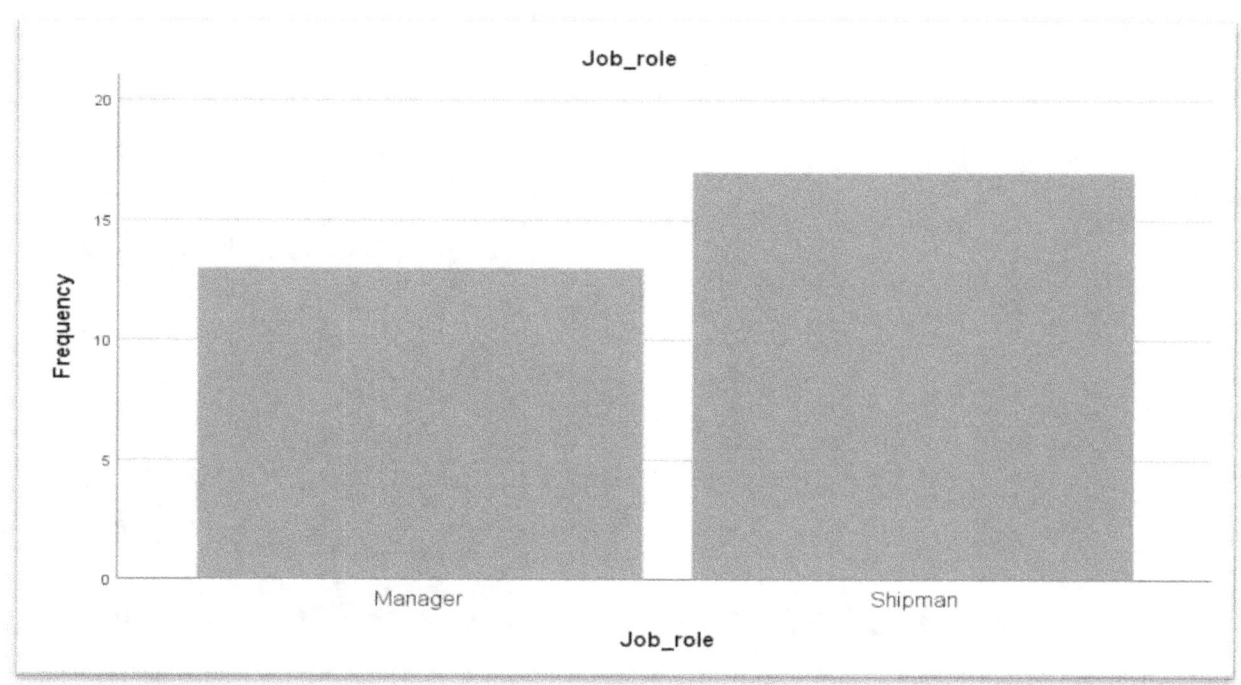

Figure 2 Bar Graph of Job Role

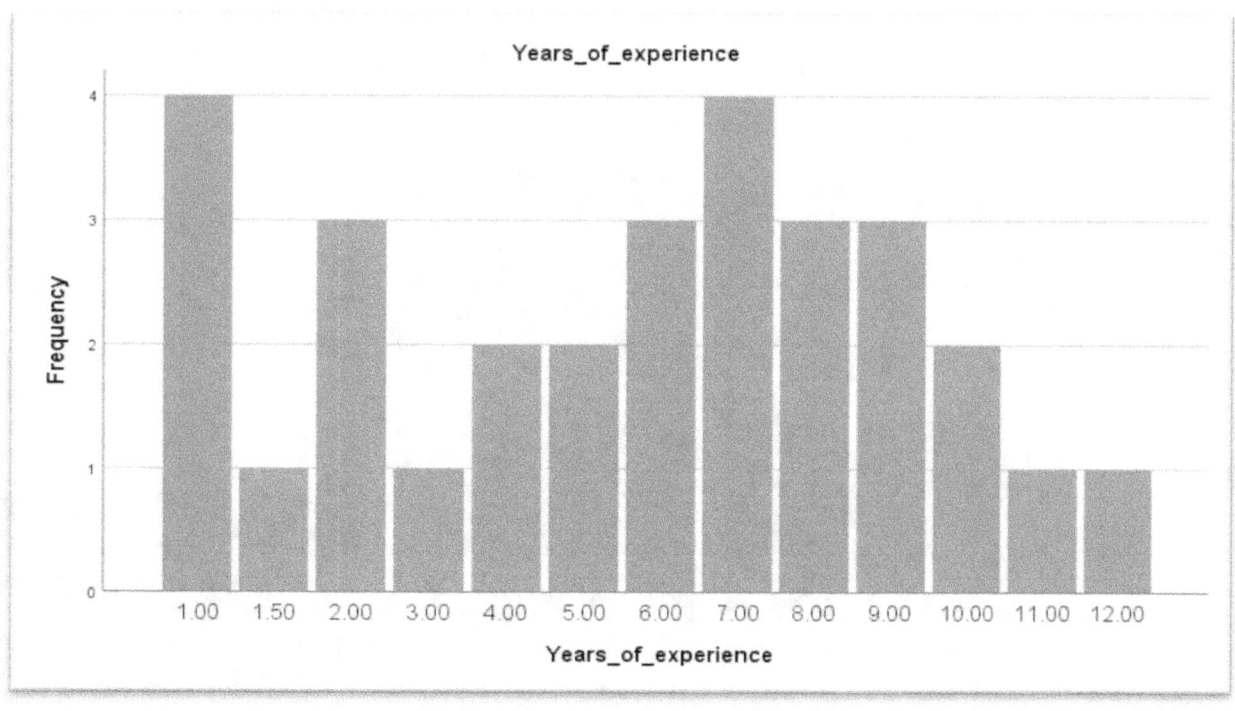

Figure 3 Bar Graph by Gender, Age, and Level of Education

49

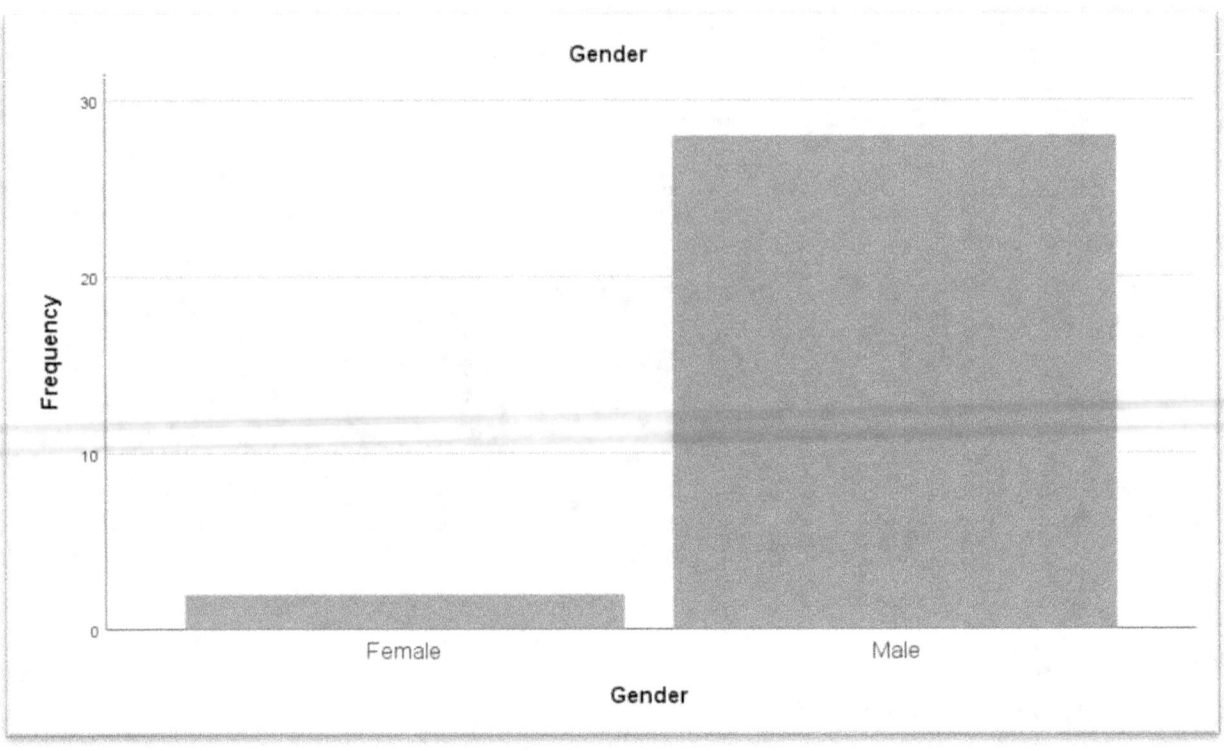

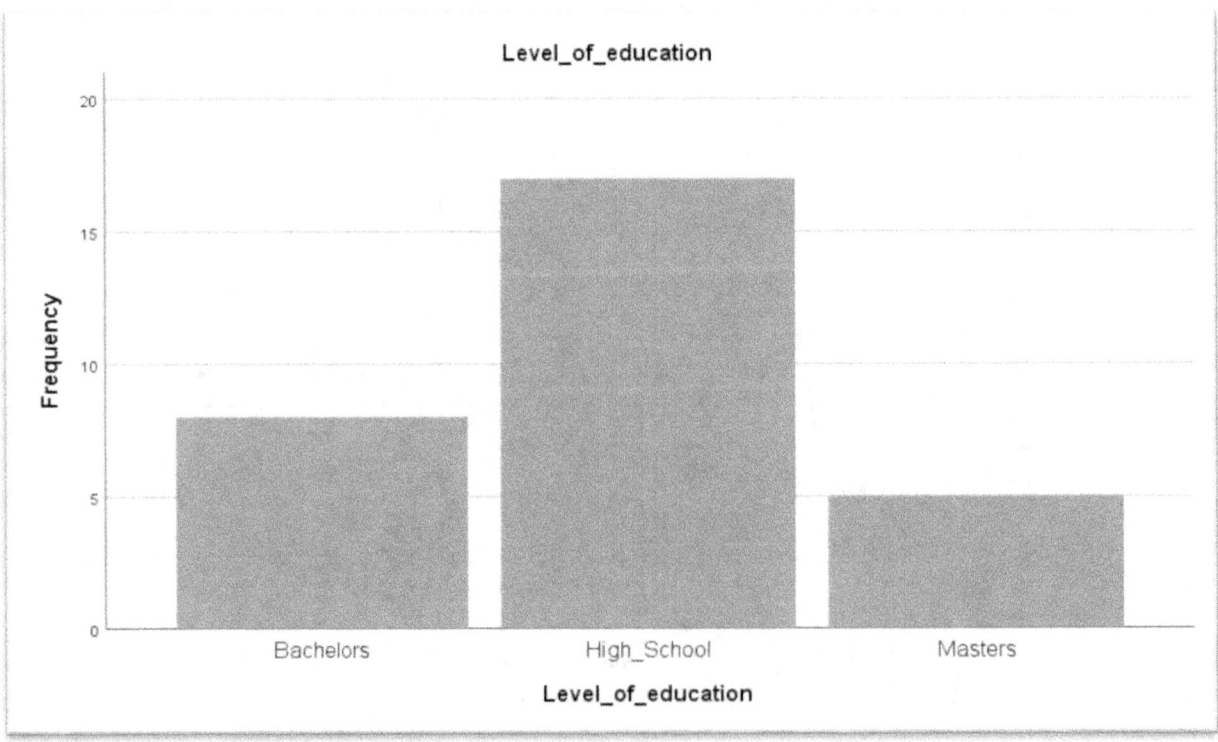

Now the t-test is conducted on dependent and independent variables as presented in the table 5. The results of t-test are as follows:

Group Statistics

	Gender	N	Mean	Std. Deviation	Std. Error Mean
dep1	Male	28	1.5000	.74536	.14086
	Female	2	2.0000	.00000	.00000
dep2	Male	28	1.3214	.86297	.16309
	Female	2	2.0000	.00000	.00000
Indep	Male	28	.1429	.35635	.06734
	Female	2	.5000	.70711	.50000

Independent Samples Test

		Levene's Test for Equality of Variances		t-test for Equality of Means					95% Confidence Interval of the Difference	
		F	Sig.	T	DF	Sig. (2-tailed)	Mean Difference	Std. Error Difference	Lower	Upper
dep1	Equal variances assumed	6.300	.018	-.933	28	.359	-.50000	.53571	-1.59736	.59736
	Equal variances not assumed			-3.550	27.000	.001	-.50000	.14086	-.78902	-.21098
dep2	Equal variances assumed	9.620	.004	-1.094	28	.283	-.67857	.62024	-1.94908	.59194
	Equal variances not assumed			-4.161	27.000	.000	-.67857	.16309	-1.01319	-.34395
Indep	Equal variances assumed	1.944	.174	-1.303	28	.203	-.35714	.27416	-.91874	.20445
	Equal variances not assumed			-.708	1.037	.604	-.35714	.50451	-6.25675	5.54247

Table 8 T-test Results

The significance level, i.e., the value of p is greater than 0.05, which suggests that the alternate hypothesis is true and there is a need for green shipping practices to be implemented. Moreover, this section also highlighted the fact that green shipping practices must be endorsed as they are the source of environmental stability, and to implement it, there is a need for LNG bunkering, shore power, and specific times for shipping to optimize the consumption of energy and shipping fuel. Furthermore, the participants believe that shore power is only established at 6.7%. They also believe that it is due to cost increases and reduced shipping that Greek ports do not make use of shore power. Another aspect inferred from this data is that LNG bunkering is not implemented at Greek ports due to maintenance issues and leakage spills of LNG. Lastly, the participants believe that LNG bunkering is only established at 3.5%. This implies that there is a significant impact of LNG bunkering and shore power on maritime energy management, which is yet not established at Greek ports. Thus, there is a need for more work by the maritime industry to ensure the sustainability of the environment. To affirm these results further ANOVA variance test is applied on the data collected in table 5. The results of ANOVA variance test are as follows:

Descriptives

			Std. Deviation	Std. Error	95% Confidence Interval for Mean		Between-Component Variance
					Lower Bound	Upper Bound	
Group1	Model	Fixed Effects	.84177	.15368	2.7185	3.3481	
		Random Effects		.24465	-.0752	6.1419	.05017
Group2	Model	Fixed Effects	.77828	.14209	2.9423	3.5244	
		Random Effects		.41985	-2.1014	8.5680	.21611

Anova

		Sum of Squares	df	Mean Square	F	Sig.
Group1	Between Groups	1.127	1	1.127	1.590	.218
	Within Groups	19.840	28	.709		
	Total	**20.967**	**29**			
Group2	Between Groups	2.407	1	2.407	3.973	.056
	Within Groups	16.960	28	.606		
	Total	19.367	29			

Table 9 ANOVA results

This also suggests that the value of p is greater than the significance value, which implies that the alternate hypothesis is correct. This infers that currently Greek ports do not have optimized green marine practices and they need to endorse LNG bunkering and shore power.

The means plots of ANOVA test are:

Figure 4 ANOVA Variance Plots

Thematic Categorical Coding

Now, the final section of additional comments is assessed where two participants have implied that green practices must be ensured for the sustainability of the environment and there is a need to protect the marine life and its pollution must be catered through effective green practices to maintain a positive impact on the marine system. Other themes derived from the research include LNG bunkering and shore power to ensure that maritime energy management is composed of green practices. These themes are illustrated below.

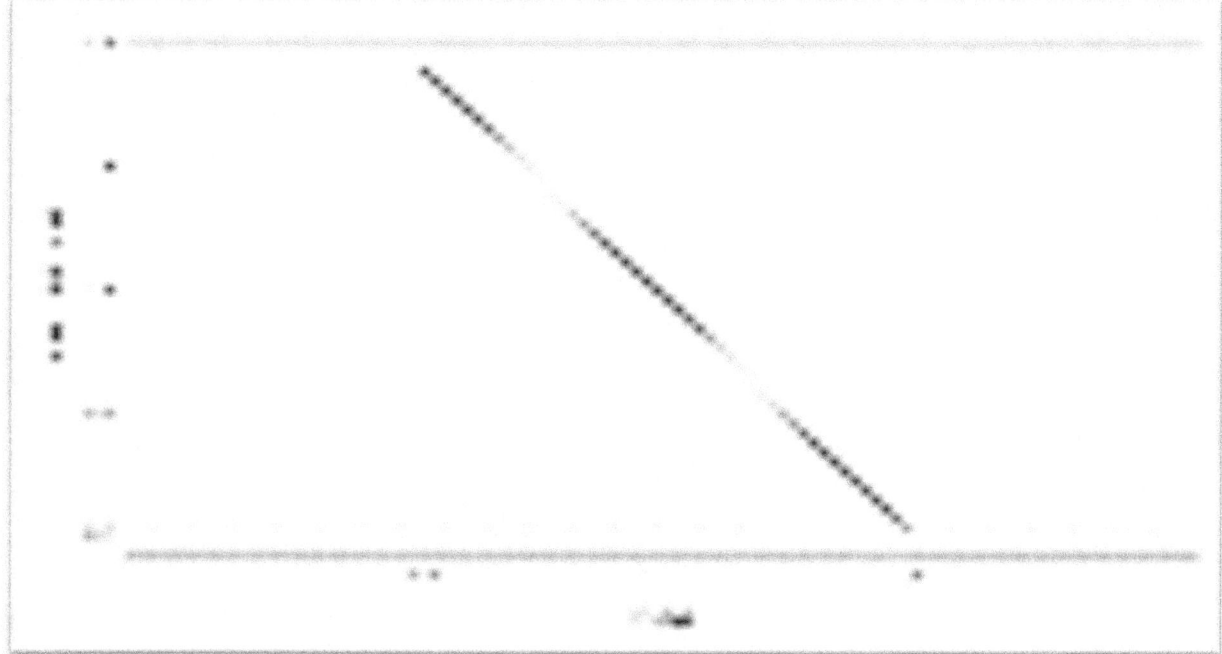

Figure 5 Themes of Research

Summary

In a nutshell, this chapter has explained all about the primary research where data collection is shown, followed by data compilation and analysis. It is proven that the alternate hypothesis is correct, and the Greek ports currently not practicing enough green practices need to change their working style at marine management. The following is an explication of the findings, their interpretation, limitations, recommendations, implications, and conclusions of the study.

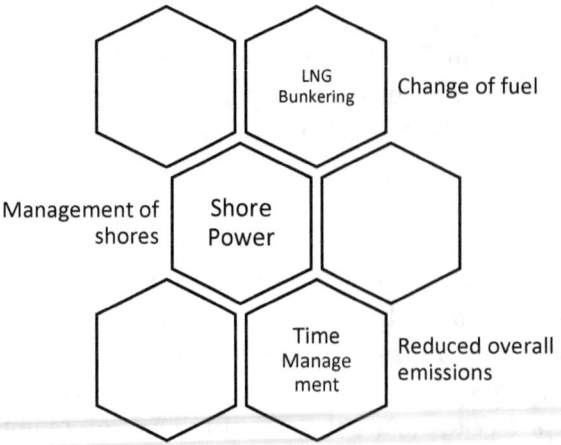

Chapter 5

Discussion, Conclusions, and Recommendations

This chapter includes a detailed discussion based on the interpretation of findings along with limitations, recommendations, and implications. Each of the findings elucidated till now is summarized in this section.

Interpretation of Findings

The findings of this research are composed of secondary findings from the literature review along with primary analysis of data collected from the survey. The review is performed through an overview of research articles associated with the efficacy of green practices at Greek ports for maritime energy management. The research has various themes and case studies highlighting the importance of collaboration, communication, knowledge sharing, and human capital to effectively implement green practices. Additionally, it emphasizes the significance of decision-making processes and adherence to international standards to optimize energy management strategies. In this review, the concept of green shipping practices, including their evolution during the COVID-19 pandemic and the need for considering broader safety and sustainability aspects. The research review also discussed the role of green marketing at major ports worldwide and its potential to attract sustainability-conscious customers. Furthermore, the review delves into the efficiency of green shipping practices that expound on carbon energy transition indicators, biofuel production, circular economy adoption, and the use of ammonia as an alternative fuel within the maritime industry. It accentuates the importance of holistically addressing environmental, social, and economic dimensions. Moreover, the annexation of various case studies from Greece enhances practical insights into waste management, water scarcity, small-scale fisheries, and the role of local and regional authorities in sustainable development. However, the review identified a research gap related to the efficacy of green practices at Greek ports, specifically to prevent excessive shore power use and promote increased LNG utilization. This gap suggested further research to investigate and address these specific aspects of maritime energy management at Greek ports. So, this literature review provides a comprehensive foundation to understand the current state of research in this field, underscoring areas where additional investigation is warranted. In addition to the secondary review, the primary analysis is also conducted by the use of a t-test and ANOVA variance test. The research sample consisted of 43.3% managers and 56.7% shipmen where this distribution represents the occupational diversity within the maritime industry. The experience levels of the participants were varied with a range from 1 to 12 years where the majority (13.3%) had 1 to 7 years of experience. Moreover, the participants were evenly distributed geographically across different Greek ports where each represent 20% of the sample. This sample was predominantly male i.e., 93.3% and have covered a wide range of ages. Additionally, education levels were varied with 56.7% held high school diplomas, 26.7% had bachelor's degrees, and 16.7% held master's degrees. Then, t-tests and ANOVA tests were implemented to examine the impact of independent variables on the dependent variable. The significance level (p-value) was found to be greater than 0.05, which suggested that the alternate hypothesis is true. This implied that there is a need to implement green shipping practices. In this case, the opinions of participants reflected that certain green shipping practices like LNG bunkering and shore power are not well-established at Greek ports. Furthermore, concerns were raised about the reasons behind the lack of adoption of these practices. For shore power, cost increases and reduced shipping were perceived as barriers, whereas maintenance issues and leakage spills were stated for LNG bunkering. The research implication suggests that there is a significant impact of LNG bunkering and shore power on maritime energy management, where these practices are not yet fully established at Greek ports. Additionally, the p-value greater than the significance level indicates that the alternate hypothesis supporting the need to endorse LNG bunkering and shore power is correct. So, it is recommended that Greek ports and the maritime industry as a whole should consider the implementation of LNG bunkering and shore power for optimizing energy consumption and reducing environmental impact. Furthermore, there is a need to adder cost concerns, maintenance issues, and safety measures for these practices should be a priority for encouraging their adoption. Hence, these practices are aligned with green shipping and sustainability goals that can contribute to a more environmentally friendly maritime industry.

Limitations of the Study

While this study provides valuable insights into the present condition of green shipping practices and maritime energy management at Greek ports, it is essential to acknowledge several limitations that can impact the generalizability and robustness of the findings. Firstly, the sample size of the study though it provides a diverse representation of managers and shipmen from different Greek ports. However, it cannot be fully representative of the entire maritime industry in Greece. The majority of participants had relatively short to moderate levels of experience that could affect their perspectives on green practices. Moreover, the study predominantly includes male participants that reflects the gender imbalance in the maritime sector and cannot fully capture the views and experiences of women working in this industry. It also manifests that there still exists a bias in hiring women at the marine management, which is a source of gender discrimination. Additionally, the data collected is self-reported and subject to potential response bias. It is because participants can provide socially desirable answers or their perceptions do not fully align with the actual practices at their respective ports. Furthermore, the study primarily relies on quantitative methods, including statistical tests like t-tests and ANOVA providing valuable insights. These test may not fully capture the nuanced qualitative aspects of participants' attitudes and experiences. The study also assumes that the participants accurately represent the reasons for the lack of adoption of LNG bunkering and shore power at Greek ports, without further verification from port authorities or other stakeholders. However, this stance is proven and verified through the research review. Lastly, the study focuses on specific green shipping practices and their influence on energy management. However, it does not delve into the broader economic, social, and policy contexts that could influence the adoption of these practices in the Greek maritime industry. Irrespective of these limitations, this research serves as a valuable starting point to understand the current state of green practices at Greek ports while highlighting the need for further research and practical interventions to promote sustainability and environmental responsibility in the maritime sector.

Recommendations

There are several recommendations that can be made for the future of maritime energy management, along with the adoption of emerging techniques to enhance sustainability and energy efficiency in the Greek maritime industry. The first recommendation is to promote collaboration and knowledge sharing through stakeholder cooperation and communication in green maritime practices (Jović et al., 2020). It is important to foster collaboration between Greek ports, shipping companies, and other relevant parties where they should establish forums or platforms for information exchange and best practices sharing to facilitate the successful implementation of green shipping initiatives. The second recommendation is to invest in professional education and training to recognize the vital role of well-trained personnel in driving energy efficiency improvements, where Greek ports should invest in education and training programs for their workforce. This will ensure that employees have the necessary skills and knowledge for adopting and implementing green practices effectively. Thirdly, there is a need to implement LNG bunkering, a green shipping practice that can potentially reduce emissions (Coimbatore Meenakshi Sundaram & Karimi, 2023). Greek ports should consider investment in the infrastructure and safety measures required for LNG bunkering operations to address concerns related to maintenance issues and LNG spills. There is also a need to expand shore power infrastructure where the ports should consider the economic and environmental benefits of shore power, such as reduced emissions and noise pollution, and work to overcome barriers that include cost increases and reduced shipping. Moreover, Greek ports should prioritize adherence to established international standards and regulations like TR 56 and IMO regulations for ensuring safe and environmentally responsible bunkering practices. There is also a need to optimize energy management and reduce emissions, where Greek ports should explore the integration of renewable energy sources. In this regard, solar panels, wind turbines, and other sustainable energy solutions can assist ports to meet their energy needs while diminishing their carbon footprint. Another recommendation is to invest in proper waste management within ports, which can contribute to environmental sustainability through the use of waste sorting and recycling programs. Moreover, the Greek maritime industry should encourage research and innovation in green shipping practices where collaboration with academic institutions and research organizations can lead to the development of new technologies and strategies to enhance sustainability. Greek ports should also actively engage with government authorities to promote policy initiatives that incentivize and support green practices. This can include financial incentives, tax breaks, and regulatory frameworks that are a source of encouraging sustainable maritime operations. Furthermore, before implementation of any significant change, the Greek ports should conduct thorough environmental impact assessments. These assessments can assist in identifying potential ecological risks and developing mitigation strategies. Another recommendation is to reduce dependency on conventional fuels. Greek ports should explore and invest in alternative fuel sources, such as biofuels. The review findings suggest that biofuels can be a source of sustainability and low-carbon energy solutions for the maritime sector. Lastly, there is a need to adopt circular economy practices that can lead to increased energy and resource efficiency. Henceforth, these recommendations are affirmed in light of literature review and primary findings to guide Greek ports and the wider maritime industry in their efforts to enhance sustainability, energy management, and environmental responsibility.

Implications

The research's implications are regarding the efficacy of green practices at Greek ports for maritime energy management. These multi-faceted practices hold significance for various stakeholders, including port authorities, shipping companies, policymakers, and the wider maritime industry. These implications circumscribe environmental sustainability, economic benefits, regulatory compliance, and the requirement for strategic planning and collaboration. First and foremost, the research accentuates the paramount significance of environmental sustainability in the maritime sector. The research findings underscore that green shipping practices like LNG bunkering, shore power utilization, and the adoption of renewable energy sources are not mere options but essential strategies to reduce greenhouse gas emissions and mitigate the environmental impact of maritime operations. Greek ports, such as many ports worldwide, face increased pressure to align with global efforts to combat climate change and meet international emissions reduction targets. So, it is clear that Greek ports must prioritize and accelerate the adoption of green practices to ensure a sustainable and environmentally responsible future. Furthermore, the research findings carry economic implications where the initial investments are required to implement green technologies and infrastructure that impact the long-term economic benefits. Moreover, reduced fuel consumption, lower emissions-related costs, and improved energy efficiency contribute towards cost savings for both port operators and shipping companies. Additionally, by embracing sustainability, Greek ports can attract environmentally conscious customers and shipping partners, bolstering their competitiveness while potentially increasing revenue. The research explicates that sustainability and economic viability are not mutually exclusive, but they go hand in hand, which promotes the idea that green practices are not only environmentally responsible but are also financially prudent. In terms of regulatory compliance, the research underscores the necessity for Greek ports to align with international standards and regulations. Furthermore, adherence to established guidelines is essential to ensure safe and environmentally responsible bunkering practices, especially in the case of LNG bunkering. In addition, non-compliance can result in legal and reputational consequences, which can adversely affect the operations and relationships of ports with shipping companies. This implies that Greek ports must prioritize regulatory compliance as an integral part of their sustainability efforts. Another implication is that strategic planning and collaboration are important for green maritime practices involving intricate sociotechnical dynamics revealed in the literature review. Moreover, effective implementation requires not only technological investments but also cooperation, communication, and knowledge sharing among various stakeholders that are composed of port authorities, shipping companies, and government bodies. Therefore, Greek ports must engage in strategic planning that can foster collaboration and information exchange. Finally, the research underscores the need for continuous research and innovation in the maritime industry. Greek ports should encourage and support research efforts to develop and optimize green technologies and strategies. In this case, collaboration with academic institutions and research organizations can lead to the discovery of new solutions that can further enhance the industry's environmental performance and energy efficiency. Henceforth, the implications of this research extend far beyond the immediate findings and touch upon critical aspects of sustainability, economics, regulation, collaboration, and innovation where Greek ports must heed these implications to ensure a greener, more sustainable, and economically viable future.

Conclusion

In conclusion, the research findings on the efficacy of green practices at Greek ports for maritime energy management provide a comprehensive and insightful overview of the current state of sustainability efforts in the Greek maritime industry. These findings shed light on several critical aspects essential for the future of industry, including environmental sustainability, economic viability, regulatory compliance, strategic planning, collaboration, and innovation. One of the primary conclusions drawn from this research is the pressing need for Greek ports to prioritize environmental sustainability since the maritime sector is under increasing scrutiny to reduce its carbon footprint and mitigate the environmental impact of its operations. The findings make it clear that green shipping practices like LNG bunkering, shore power utilization, and the adoption of renewable energy sources are not just desirable but imperative for Greek ports. These practices contribute to reducing greenhouse gas emissions and position Greek ports as responsible units towards environmental stewards. Moreover, economic implications also emerge as a key conclusion where initial investments are required to implement green technologies and infrastructure. In this case, the long-term economic benefits are substantial, where the research demonstrates that green practices can lead to cost savings through reduced fuel consumption and lower emissions-related expenses. Furthermore, implementing sustainability suggests that Greek ports can enhance their attractiveness to environmentally conscious customers and shipping partners, bolstering their competitiveness and potential for increased revenue. Thus, the conclusion is that green practices not only coincide with environmental goals but also instill an economic sense. It is also found that regulatory compliance is essential as Greek ports must adhere to established international standards and regulations for ensuring safety and environmentally responsible bunkering practices, especially in the case of LNG bunkering. It is also implicated that non-compliance can result in legal and reputational consequences, underscoring the necessity for Greek ports to prioritize regulatory alignment as an integral part of their sustainability efforts. Another conclusion is that strategic planning and collaboration emerge as imperative where green maritime practices involve complex sociotechnical dynamics, and effective implementation requires not only technological investments but also cooperation, communication, and knowledge sharing among various stakeholders. The research underscores the importance of Greek ports in engaging in strategic planning that fosters collaboration and information exchange. Lastly, the research findings emphasize the need for continuous research and innovation within the maritime industry, where Greek ports should actively support and participate in research efforts aimed at collaboration with academic institutions and research organizations that can lead to the discovery of new solutions. This helps in further enhancing the environmental performance and energy efficiency of the industry. Henceforth, the research findings serve as a clarion call to Greek ports and the wider maritime industry, where they provide a roadmap toward a greener, more sustainable, and economically viable future.

References

Adamowicz, M. (2022). Decarbonisation of maritime transport–European Union measures as an inspiration for global solutions? *Marine Policy*, *145*, 105085. https://doi.org/10.1016/j.marpol.2022.105085

Adedoyin, F. F., Erum, N., & Bekun, F. V. (2022). How does institutional quality moderates the impact of tourism on economic growth? Startling evidence from high earners and tourism-dependent economies. *Tourism Economics*, *28*(5), 1311–1332.

Al-Enazi, A., Okonkwo, E. C., Bicer, Y., & Al-Ansari, T. (2021). A review of cleaner alternative fuels for maritime transportation. *Energy Reports*, *7*, 1962–1985.

Anastasiu, L., Gavriş, O., & Maier, D. (2020). Is Human Capital Ready for Change? A Strategic Approach Adapting Porter's Five Forces to Human Resources. *Sustainability*, *12*(6), Article 6. https://doi.org/10.3390/su12062300

Argyriou, I., Daras, T., & Tsoutsos, T. (2022). Challenging a sustainable port. A case study of Souda port, Chania, Crete. *Case Studies on Transport Policy*, *10*(4), 2125–2137.

Asmus, E. P., & Radocy, R. E. (2012). Quantitative Analysis. In *Critical Essays in Music Education*. Routledge.

Axel, B. N. (2011). *Environmental impacts of international shipping the role of ports: The role of ports* (Vol. 2011). OECD Publishing.

Babii, A. (2020). Important aspects of the experimental research methodology. *Вісник Тернопільського Національного Технічного Університету*, *97*(1), 77–87.

Ball, H. L. (2019). Conducting online surveys. *Journal of Human Lactation*, *35*(3), 413–417.

Banias, G., Batsioula, M., Achillas, C., Patsios, S. I., Kontogiannopoulos, K. N., Bochtis, D., & Moussiopoulos, N. (2020). A Life Cycle Analysis Approach for the Evaluation of Municipal Solid Waste Management Practices: The Case Study of the Region of Central Macedonia, Greece. *Sustainability*, *12*(19), Article 19. https://doi.org/10.3390/su12198221

Becker, T. E., Atinc, G., Breaugh, J. A., Carlson, K. D., Edwards, J. R., & Spector, P. E. (2016). Statistical control in correlational studies: 10 essential recommendations for organizational researchers. *Journal of Organizational Behavior*, *37*(2), 157–167.

Bhandari, P. (2021). A guide to ethical considerations in research. *Scribbr. Retrieved December*, *18*, 2021.

Bintoudi, E., Baert, M., & Drakaki, M. (2020). *Ecological footprint analysis of the port of Thessaloniki as a tool for an environmental management system* (p. 51). https://doi.org/10.46354/i3m.2020.hms.007

Bonsu, N. O. (2020). Towards a circular and low-carbon economy: Insights from the transitioning to electric vehicles and net zero economy. *Journal of Cleaner Production*, *256*, 120659. https://doi.org/10.1016/j.jclepro.2020.120659

Bordoff, J., & O'Sullivan Meghan, L. (2022). Green upheaval: The new geopolitics of energy. *Foreign Aff.*, *101*, 68.

Brunila, O.-P., Kunnaala-Hyrkki, V., & Inkinen, T. (2023). Sustainable small ports: Performance assessment tool for management, responsibility, impact, and self-monitoring. *Journal of Shipping and Trade*, *8*(1), 1–24.

Coimbatore Meenakshi Sundaram, A., & Karimi, I. A. (2023). Sustainability Analysis of an LNG Bunkering Protocol. *ACS Sustainable Chemistry & Engineering*. https://doi.org/10.1021/acssuschemeng.3c02914

de Kat, J. O., & Mouawad, J. (2019). Green ship technologies. *Sustainable Shipping: A Cross-Disciplinary View*, 33–92.

Delios, A., Clemente, E. G., Wu, T., Tan, H., Wang, Y., Gordon, M., Viganola, D., Chen, Z., Dreber, A., & Johannesson, M. (2022). Examining the generalizability of research findings from archival data. *Proceedings of the National Academy of Sciences*, *119*(30), e2120377119.

Delis, A. (2022). The Advent of Steam Navigation in Greece in the Nineteenth Century. In *Greek Maritime History* (pp. 191–231). Brill. https://doi.org/10.1163/9789004467729_010

Dey, P. K., Malesios, C., Chowdhury, S., Saha, K., Budhwar, P., & De, D. (2022). Adoption of circular economy practices in small and medium-sized enterprises: Evidence from Europe. *International Journal of Production Economics*, *248*, 108496. https://doi.org/10.1016/j.ijpe.2022.108496

Dimnwobi, S. K., Nwokoye, E. S., Igbanugo, C. I., Ekesiobi, C. S., & Asongu, S. A. (2023). Assessment of energy efficiency investment in Onitsha business cluster, Nigeria. *International Journal of Energy Sector Management*.

Egbert, J., Biber, D., & Gray, B. (2022). *Designing and evaluating language corpora: A practical framework for corpus representativeness*. Cambridge University Press.

Fan, H., Enshaei, H., & Gamini Jayasinghe, S. (2021). Safety philosophy and risk analysis methodology for LNG bunkering simultaneous operations (SIMOPs): A literature review. *Safety Science*, *136*, 105150. https://doi.org/10.1016/j.ssci.2020.105150

Fang, S., & Wang, H. (2021). *Optimization-based energy management for multi-energy maritime grids*. Springer Nature.

Galiatsatou, P., Makris, C., Krestenitis, Y., & Prinos, P. (2021). Nonstationary Extreme Value Analysis of Nearshore Sea-State Parameters under the Effects of Climate Change: Application to the Greek Coastal Zone and Port Structures. *Journal of Marine Science and Engineering*, *9*(8), Article 8. https://doi.org/10.3390/jmse9080817

Gerald, B. (2018). A brief review of independent, dependent and one sample t-test. *International Journal of Applied Mathematics and Theoretical Physics*, *4*(2), 50–54.

Gössling, S., Meyer-Habighorst, C., & Humpe, A. (2021). A global review of marine air pollution policies, their scope and effectiveness. *Ocean & Coastal Management*, *212*, 105824.

Gras, S. (2013). *Hierarchical information retreival and boolean search strings* (United States Patent US20130091113A1). https://patents.google.com/patent/US20130091113A1/en

Ha, M.-H., Park, H., & Seo, Y.-J. (2023). Understanding core determinants in LNG bunkering port selection: Policy implications for the maritime industry. *Marine Policy*, *152*, 105608. https://doi.org/10.1016/j.marpol.2023.105608

Harrell, J., & Harrell, F. E. (2015). Ordinal logistic regression. *Regression Modeling Strategies: With Applications to Linear Models, Logistic and Ordinal Regression, and Survival Analysis*, 311–325.

Heskett, J. (2022). *Win from Within: Build Organizational Culture for Competitive Advantage*. Columbia University Press.

Holian, R., & Coghlan, D. (2013). Ethical issues and role duality in insider action research: Challenges for action research degree programmes. *Systemic Practice and Action Research*, *26*, 399–415.

Holmes, A. G. D. (2020). Researcher Positionality—A Consideration of Its Influence and Place in Qualitative Research—A New Researcher Guide. *Shanlax International Journal of Education*, *8*(4), 1–10.

Hughes, A. C., Orr, M. C., Ma, K., Costello, M. J., Waller, J., Provoost, P., Yang, Q., Zhu, C., & Qiao, H. (2021). Sampling biases shape our view of the natural world. *Ecography*, *44*(9), 1259–1269.

IQAir. (2023, September 8). *Piraeus Air Quality Index (AQI) and Greece Air Pollution | IQAir*. https://www.iqair.com/greece/attica/piraeus

Iris, Ç., & Lam, J. S. L. (2019). A review of energy efficiency in ports: Operational strategies, technologies and energy management systems. *Renewable and Sustainable Energy Reviews*, *112*, 170–182. https://doi.org/10.1016/j.rser.2019.04.069

Isabelle, D., Horak, K., McKinnon, S., & Palumbo, C. (2020). Is Porter's Five Forces Framework Still Relevant? A study of the capital/labour intensity continuum via mining and IT industries. *Technology Innovation Management Review*, *10*(6), 28–41. https://doi.org/10.22215/timreview/1366

Jacyna, M., Żochowska, R., Sobota, A., & Wasiak, M. (2021). Scenario Analyses of Exhaust Emissions Reduction through the Introduction of Electric Vehicles into the City. *Energies*, *14*(7), Article 7. https://doi.org/10.3390/en14072030

Jepperson, R. L., & Meyer, J. W. (2021). *Institutional theory: The cultural construction of organizations, states, and identities*. Cambridge University Press.

Jović, M., Tijan, E., Žgaljić, D., & Aksentijević, S. (2020). Improving maritime transport sustainability using blockchain-based information exchange. *Sustainability*, *12*(21), 8866.

Jun, H., & Kim, M. (2021). From stakeholder communication to engagement for the sustainable development goals (SDGs): A case study of LG electronics. *Sustainability*, *13*(15), 8624.

Kalogiannidis, S., Chatzitheodoridis, F., Dimitrios, K., & Papadopoulou, C.-I. (2023). Role of Local and Regional Authorities in Inclusive, Resilient, and Green Recovery for Sustainable Development: Case Study of Greece. In *Financing Regions Toward Sustainability in the Midst of Climate Change Risks and Uncertainty* (pp. 1–26). IGI Global. https://doi.org/10.4018/978-1-6684-7620-8.ch001

Kaur, P., Stoltzfus, J., & Yellapu, V. (2018). Descriptive statistics. *International Journal of Academic Medicine*, *4*(1), 60.

Kim, H.-Y. (2014). Analysis of variance (ANOVA) comparing means of more than two groups. *Restorative Dentistry & Endodontics*, *39*(1), 74–77.

Konstantakopoulos, G. D., Gayialis, S. P., Kechagias, E. P., Papadopoulos, G. A., & Tatsiopoulos, I. P. (2021). An algorithmic approach for sustainable and collaborative logistics: A case study in Greece. *International Journal of Information Management Data Insights*, *1*(1), 100010. https://doi.org/10.1016/j.jjimei.2021.100010

Kowalkowski, C., Tronvoll, B., Sörhammar, D., & Sklyar, A. (2022). Digital servitization: How data-driven services drive transformation. *HICSS-55*.

Kravariti, F., Oruh, E. S., Dibia, C., Tasoulis, K., Scullion, H., & Mamman, A. (2021). Weathering the storm: Talent management in internationally oriented Greek small and medium-sized enterprises. *Journal of Organizational Effectiveness: People and Performance*, *8*(4), 444–463.

Kyvelou, S. S. I., & Ierapetritis, D. G. (2020). Fisheries Sustainability through Soft Multi-Use Maritime Spatial Planning and Local Development Co-Management: Potentials and Challenges in Greece. *Sustainability*, *12*(5), Article 5. https://doi.org/10.3390/su12052026

Lam, J. S. L., & Li, K. X. (2019). Green port marketing for sustainable growth and development. *Transport Policy*, *84*, 73–81. https://doi.org/10.1016/j.tranpol.2019.04.011

Lê, J. K., & Schmid, T. (2022). The practice of innovating research methods. *Organizational Research Methods*, *25*(2), 308–336. https://doi.org/10.1177/1094428120935498

Leary, D. (2020). 8. International Maritime Organization (IMO). *Yearbook of International Environmental Law*, *31*(1), 305–306.

Lee, P. T.-W., Kwon, O. K., & Ruan, X. (2019). Sustainability Challenges in Maritime Transport and Logistics Industry and Its Way Ahead. *Sustainability*, *11*(5), Article 5. https://doi.org/10.3390/su11051331

Leichsenring, F., Abbass, A., Hilsenroth, M. J., Leweke, F., Luyten, P., Keefe, J. R., Midgley, N., Rabung, S., Salzer, S., & Steinert, C. (2017). Biases in research: Risk factors for non-replicability in psychotherapy and pharmacotherapy research. *Psychological Medicine*, *47*(6), 1000–1011.

Leka, A., Lagarias, A., Panagiotopoulou, M., & Stratigea, A. (2022). Development of a Tourism Carrying Capacity Index (TCCI) for sustainable management of coastal areas in Mediterranean islands – Case study Naxos, Greece. *Ocean & Coastal Management*, *216*, 105978. https://doi.org/10.1016/j.ocecoaman.2021.105978

Mako, P., Dávid, A., Böhm, P., & Savu, S. (2021). Sustainable Transport in the Danube Region. *Sustainability*, *13*(12), Article 12. https://doi.org/10.3390/su13126797

Mallouppas, G., Ioannou, C., & Yfantis, E. A. (2022). A Review of the Latest Trends in the Use of Green Ammonia as an Energy Carrier in Maritime Industry. *Energies*, *15*(4), Article 4. https://doi.org/10.3390/en15041453

Martin. (2023). Climate Change. *United Nations Sustainable Development*. https://www.un.org/sustainabledevelopment/climate-change/

Mentese, S., & Selçuk, B. (2022). Assessment of ambient air quality, meteorological parameters, and emission source characteristics of Çanakkale, Turkey. *International Journal of Environmental Science and Technology*, *19*(2), 1025–1040.

Meys, R., Kätelhön, A., Bachmann, M., Winter, B., Zibunas, C., Suh, S., & Bardow, A. (2021). Achieving net-zero greenhouse gas emission plastics by a circular carbon economy. *Science*, *374*(6563), 71–76. https://doi.org/10.1126/science.abg9853

Mishra, P., Singh, U., Pandey, C. M., Mishra, P., & Pandey, G. (2019). Application of student's t-test, analysis of variance, and covariance. *Annals of Cardiac Anaesthesia*, *22*(4), 407.

Moody-Marshall, R. (2023). An investigation of environmental awareness and practice among a sample of undergraduate students in Belize. *Environmental Education Research*, *29*(7), 911–928.

Nyman, E. (2015). Offshore oil development and maritime conflict in the 20th century: A statistical analysis of international trends. *Energy Research & Social Science*, *6*, 1–7.

Ocasio, W. (2023). Institutions and Their Social Construction: A Cross-Level Perspective. *Organization Theory*, *4*(3), 26317877231194368. https://doi.org/10.1177/26317877231194368

Okagbue, H. I., Oguntunde, P. E., Obasi, E. C., & Akhmetshin, E. M. (2021). Trends and usage pattern of SPSS and Minitab Software in Scientific research. *Journal of Physics: Conference Series*, *1734*(1), 012017.

Palantzas, G., Darbra Roman, R. M., Naniopoulos, A., Tselentis, V., & Wooldridge, C. (2021). *The environmental management of small ports – challenges and options*. Proceedings Greenport 2021 Online. https://upcommons.upc.edu/handle/2117/365226

Peng, F. F. C. (2022). *Overview of the Development of Low/Zero-Emission Marine Fuels and Implications for China.*

Pickering, D., & Blaszczynski, A. (2021). Paid online convenience samples in gambling studies: Questionable data quality. *International Gambling Studies, 21*(3), 516–536.

Platias, C., & Spyrou, D. (2023). EU-Funded Energy-Related Projects for Sustainable Ports: Evidence from the Port of Piraeus. *Sustainability, 15*(5), Article 5. https://doi.org/10.3390/su15054363

Porter, M. E. (2008). The five competitive forces that shape strategy. *Harvard Business Review, 86*(1), 78.

Prokopenko, O., & Miśkiewicz, R. (2020). Perception of "Green Shipping" in the contemporary conditions. *Entrepreneurship and Sustainability Issues, 8*(2), 269–284. https://doi.org/10.9770/jesi.2020.8.2(16)

Prousalidis, J., Lyridis, D., Dallas, S., Soghomonian, Z., Georgiou, V., Spathis, D., Kourmpelis, T., & Mitrou, P. (2017). Ship to shore electric interconnection: From adolescence to maturity. *2017 IEEE Electric Ship Technologies Symposium (ESTS),* 200–206.

Puig, M., Azarkamand, S., Wooldridge, C., Selén, V., & Darbra, R. M. (2022). Insights on the environmental management system of the European port sector. *Science of The Total Environment, 806,* 150550. https://doi.org/10.1016/j.scitotenv.2021.150550

Qi, J., Wang, S., & Peng, C. (2020). Shore power management for maritime transportation: Status and perspectives. *Maritime Transport Research, 1,* 100004. https://doi.org/10.1016/j.martra.2020.100004

Rebelo, P. (2020). Green Finance for a Sustainable Maritime Transport System: Developing a Universal Vernacular for Green Shipping. *Australian and New Zealand Maritime Law Journal, 34,* 15.

Rocha, C. S., Antunes, P., & Partidário, P. (2019). Design for sustainability models: A multiperspective review. *Journal of Cleaner Production, 234,* 1428–1445. https://doi.org/10.1016/j.jclepro.2019.06.108

Roopa, S., & Rani, M. S. (2012). Questionnaire designing for a survey. *Journal of Indian Orthodontic Society, 46*(4_suppl1), 273–277.

Sarker, M., & AL-Muaalemi, M. A. (2022). Sampling techniques for quantitative research. In *Principles of Social Research Methodology* (pp. 221–234). Springer.

Scott, G. (2020). *Porter's 5 Forces.* Investopedia. https://www.investopedia.com/terms/p/porter.asp

Sdoukopoulos, E., Boile, M., Tromaras, A., & Anastasiadis, N. (2019). Energy efficiency in European ports: State-of-practice and insights on the way forward. *Sustainability, 11*(18), 4952.

Sedgwick, P. (2013). Convenience sampling. *Bmj, 347.*

Serra, P., & Fancello, G. (2020). Towards the IMO's GHG goals: A critical overview of the perspectives and challenges of the main options for decarbonizing international shipping. *Sustainability, 12*(8), 3220.

Shah, P., Thornton, I., Turrin, D., & Hipskind, J. E. (2022). Informed Consent. In *StatPearls.* StatPearls Publishing. http://www.ncbi.nlm.nih.gov/books/NBK430827/

Sideri, O., Papoutsidakis, M., Lilas, T., Nikitakos, N., & Papachristos, D. (2021). Green shipping onboard: Acceptance, diffusion & adoption of LNG and electricity as alternative fuels in Greece. *Journal of Shipping and Trade, 6,* 1–29.

Sileyew, K. J. (2019). Research design and methodology. *Cyberspace,* 1–12.

Silva-Rêgo, B., & Figueira, A. (2023). Institutional theory and outward foreign direct investment: A review and future directions. *European Journal of International Management*, *21*(1), 55–95. https://doi.org/10.1504/EJIM.2023.132794

Smith, L. H. (2020). Selection mechanisms and their consequences: Understanding and addressing selection bias. *Current Epidemiology Reports*, *7*, 179–189.

Spanuth, A., & Urbano, D. (2023). Exploring social enterprise legitimacy within ecosystems from an institutional approach: A systematic literature review and research agenda. *International Journal of Management Reviews*.

Stratton, S. J. (2021). Population research: Convenience sampling strategies. *Prehospital and Disaster Medicine*, *36*(4), 373–374.

Streimikiene, D., Kyriakopoulos, G. L., Lekavicius, V., & Siksnelyte-Butkiene, I. (2021). Energy Poverty and Low Carbon Just Energy Transition: Comparative Study in Lithuania and Greece. *Social Indicators Research*, *158*(1), 319–371. https://doi.org/10.1007/s11205-021-02685-9

Suganthi, L. (2019). Examining the relationship between corporate social responsibility, performance, employees' pro-environmental behavior at work with green practices as mediator. *Journal of Cleaner Production*, *232*, 739–750.

Tang, C.-S., Paleologos, E. K., Vitone, C., Du, Y.-J., Li, J.-S., Jiang, N.-J., Deng, Y.-F., Chu, J., Shen, Z., Koda, E., Dominijanni, A., Fei, X., Vaverková, M. D., Osiński, P., Chen, X., Asadi, A., Takeuchi, M. R. H., Bo, M. W., Abuel-Naga, H., … Singh, D. N. (2021). Environmental geotechnics: Challenges and opportunities in the post-Covid-19 world. *Environmental Geotechnics*, *8*(3), 172–192. https://doi.org/10.1680/jenge.20.00054

Testa, D. (2020). A note on the potential designation of the mediterranean sea as a sulphur emission control area. *Marine Policy*, *121*, 104145.

Tsita, K. G., Kiartzis, S. J., Ntavos, N. K., & Pilavachi, P. A. (2020). Next generation biofuels derived from thermal and chemical conversion of the Greek transport sector. *Thermal Science and Engineering Progress*, *17*, 100387. https://doi.org/10.1016/j.tsep.2019.100387

Tvedten, I. Ø., & Bauer, S. (2022). Retrofitting towards a greener marine shipping future: Reassembling ship fuels and liquefied natural gas in Norway. *Energy Research & Social Science*, *86*, 102423.

Tzanakakis, V. A., Angelakis, A. N., Paranychianakis, N. V., Dialynas, Y. G., & Tchobanoglous, G. (2020). Challenges and Opportunities for Sustainable Management of Water Resources in the Island of Crete, Greece. *Water*, *12*(6), Article 6. https://doi.org/10.3390/w12061538

Vagiona, D. G. (2021). Comparative Multicriteria Analysis Methods for Ranking Sites for Solar Farm Deployment: A Case Study in Greece. *Energies*, *14*(24), Article 24. https://doi.org/10.3390/en14248371

Viktorelius, M., Varvne, H., & von Knorring, H. (2022). An overview of sociotechnical research on maritime energy efficiency. *WMU Journal of Maritime Affairs*, *21*(3), 387–399. https://doi.org/10.1007/s13437-022-00263-5

Visvardis, G. (2019). *Green ports: The case of Greek ports* [Master Thesis, Πανεπιστήμιο Πειραιώς]. https://dione.lib.unipi.gr/xmlui/handle/unipi/12302

Wu, L., & Wang, S. (2020). The shore power deployment problem for maritime transportation. *Transportation Research Part E: Logistics and Transportation Review*, *135*, 101883.

Xu, L., Di, Z., Chen, J., Shi, J., & Yang, C. (2021). Evolutionary game analysis on behavior strategies of multiple stakeholders in maritime shore power system. *Ocean & Coastal Management*, *202*, 105508. https://doi.org/10.1016/j.ocecoaman.2020.105508

Zannis, T. C., Katsanis, J. S., Christopoulos, G. P., Yfantis, E. A., Papagiannakis, R. G., Pariotis, E. G., Rakopoulos, D. C., Rakopoulos, C. D., & Vallis, A. G. (2022). Marine exhaust gas treatment systems for compliance with the IMO 2020 global sulfur cap and tier III NOx limits: A review. *Energies, 15*(10), 3638.

www.ingramcontent.com/pod-product-compliance
Lightning Source LLC
Chambersburg PA
CBHW080851120626
46546CB00008B/2785

9781963159066